SECRET DOUBTS

Working through Unspoken Unbelief

Tim Zacharias

Originally published as *Working through an Asaph Moment* in 2013. Published in 2016 by Striving Together Publications, a ministry of Lancaster Baptist Church, Lancaster, CA 93535. Striving Together Publications is committed to providing tried, trusted, and proven books that will further equip local churches to carry out the Great Commission. Your comments and suggestions are valued.

Striving Together Publications
4020 E. Lancaster Blvd.
Lancaster, CA 93535
800.201.7748

Cover design by Andrew Jones
Edited by Monica Bass
Layout by Craig Parker

The author and publication team have put forth every effort to give proper credit to quotes and thoughts that are not original with the author. It is not our intent to claim originality with any quote or thought that could not readily be tied to an original source.

ISBN 978-1-59894-325-2
Printed in the United States of America

DEDICATION

I dedicate this book to my lovely wife, Stacie. She has been my partner in life and in ministry. Her strength and support have been a mainstay for me through the many ups and downs of life. I love you, Stacie!

CONTENTS

FOREWORD vii

PREFACE—Asaph and I ix

ONE—Disillusioned. 1

TWO—God Is Good, But— 7

THREE—Am I the Exception?. 17

FOUR—Why Them? 25

FIVE—Does God Really Know? 33

SIX—What's the Use? 41

SEVEN—Secret Doubts 49

EIGHT—The Sanctuary Revelation 55

NINE—The Retribution of the Wicked 65

TEN—I'm as Dumb as an Ox! 75

ELEVEN—The Reward of the Righteous. . . . 83

TWELVE—It's All Good! 93

ACKNOWLEDGMENTS 101

FOREWORD

I have had the privilege of knowing Tim and Stacie Zacharias for close to twelve years. Not only are we close friends, but we are also ministry partners. Tim and I are both church planters and pastors. Both of us left secure positions in larger ministries to venture to New England to start separate churches from scratch. It is here that we first met, and our families connected through the similarities in our children's ages, our vocation, and our ministry experiences.

I have come to admire Tim as a fellow pastor for advice in times of decisions, for his knowledge of the Scriptures in discussing doctrine, and for watching his family face trials that would cause even a good man to question God. But Tim and Stacie live what they believe about their God. Tim has a clear and practical way of teaching the principles of the Bible. His ability to extract the truth from Scripture and make it applicable to the listener is desirable as a teacher. In this book, Tim does a wonderful job describing Asaph's condition and intertwining his personal story to help the reader know that others struggle with similar times of desperation. God does offer help for those times of secret doubts.

Tim's story is a fascinating one. It was at my house when Tim experienced pain in his back that put him on the floor as he tried to stretch it out. A few weeks later he called me with the news that the pain in his back was not a muscle strain, but a form of cancer that was eating holes into his spine. As I have observed the challenges that he has faced, I believe that he exhibits qualities that demonstrate a real reliance on God. Tim and Stacie are living testimonies of how God gives believers grace through trials as they trust His plan even when the burdens are not immediately lifted, and the heart grows weary under the load.

This exposition of Psalm 73 is an excellent example of Tim's ability to clearly communicate God's Word. I personally have learned much. Although he has great humor and you'll laugh while you learn, my knowledge of the days, months, and even years of personal pain that both he and his dear wife have been through has caused me to understand how God gives grace and to admire their unwavering faith. This book could be considered an exposition of Tim's life and relationship with God.

—Pastor John Ludka
Community Baptist Church in Groton, Connecticut

PREFACE

ASAPH AND I

My wife Stacie and I jokingly call it "The Zac Curse." (In case it isn't immediately obvious, Zac is short for Zacharias. We even prefer to be called the Zacs for short. It is easier to say, and it prevents us being called by the name of every other prophet in the book.) "The Zac Curse" means that anything that can go wrong usually does go wrong in our lives, especially at the most inopportune times.

This curse, so dubbed, usually manifests itself during our family vacations. For example, there was the time when we arrived at the airport for a trip to see the grandparents only to realize that we had left Stacie's luggage at home, some three and a half hours away. The plane was leaving soon and we had to go without it. Stacie's life was in that bag—everything that she needed for the trip, including many irreplaceable items. How in the world did we miss that bag? The only plan we could think of was to call our associate pastor, Matt Fitch, and tell him how he might break into our house to retrieve the lonely bag. He could "overnight" it to us. We suggested a way that he might get inside without breaking down the door or shattering glass. It was exciting and disconcerting at the same time to get a phone call from him five minutes later saying, "I'm in!" What a save! But the curse continued as we had to pay a bill for the airfreight that cost us more than a seat on our plane. (I hope the bag enjoyed the flight.)

"The Zac Curse" has become so constant that sometimes it seems as if the phrase is emblematic of our whole married life. Don't get me wrong, we are very blessed indeed. We love each other. We love our children. We have a wonderful and supportive church and extended family. We live in a great town, in a great state, and in a great country. Best of all, we have a personal, saving relationship with Jesus Christ, and we know that we are going to Heaven someday. We truly can count our blessings. But our burdens can wear at our spirits. They come like waves pounding on the seashore—regular and hard. I'm sure others have it worse than we do, but we do not know their pain as personally as we know our own. Calling our hardships a "curse" is merely a way to make light of that which would otherwise be cause for madness.

I'm hesitant to say this lest I discourage someone, but the hardships really began in earnest when we entered full-time ministry soon after we were married. There we were, serving

God with zeal and freshness, excited about the prospects ahead. I entered the youth ministry at a large church in North Carolina. It was the most challenging and rewarding thing I had ever done. Stacie was there by my side, working, ministering, and helping. Our ministry life took off, but so did the difficulties.

The first major burden came with our inability to have children. Stacie and I wanted children so badly that it hurt. We prayed and prayed for this blessing, but things did not happen as we would have hoped. Actually, we did have seven children in so many years—seven developing babies in the womb—seven miscarriages. We know that someday we will meet them in Heaven, but to a young couple ministering in the midst of many full and vibrant families, that seemed like little consolation.

In time, the dream to birth children of our own began to diminish in our minds. The bubble had burst, and it was time to move on. Adoption became the new and exciting alternative. Once we had accepted the notion that having children by natural means might not be our reality, we started to research adoption. Maybe, we thought, God could work in this way to bless us with a family. Through contacts and connections, we were able to apply and be accepted by an adoption agency. The agency we had chosen, and which had chosen us, works to place newborn babies with Christian couples like us.

While we were waiting and praying for that one life-changing phone call from the agency, the phone rang with an amazing opportunity from a different direction. A pastor friend of ours called to inform us concerning a young four-year-old boy who needed a home. At the time, this sad little child was staying with a relative. We learned in time that he was there because he had just been rejected after staying with a potential adoptive family for six months. From what we knew, they had made plans to adopt him, but it did not take long for them to realize that this boy was more than they were willing or able to handle. This couple had come to believe that he had a condition known as "Reactive Attachment Disorder" (RAD). When we pulled up to the park to meet him for the first time, something happened that could have given us a clue that there was something to these reports. When his aunt left the van to greet us, this little "RAD lad" locked himself inside and refused to come out. You should have seen the spectacle of three adults trying to coax this child into opening the door. We cajoled, bribed, and pleaded. He finally gave in, learning that there was fast food and a gift in his future. In a state of naiveté and idealism, Stacie and I said to ourselves, "All he needs is a little love and discipline, and he'll be just fine." Since then we have been living a continual nightmare. Our son has seen countless professionals and been involved in numerous programs. He has been diagnosed with multiple disorders by conflicting sources. We paid for the best treatment and help. We prayed for deliverance, but things only went from bad to worse. We came to believe that our son struggles with a developmental deficiency. He lacks the natural disposition to trust and empathize—both essential elements needed to relate well with self and others. In a spiritual sense, he has exhibited a stubborn resistance to help in any form. He is grown and on his own now. There is still hope for him, but the years of conflict can never be relived.

Through all of this pain, God blessed us with enough blessings to give us hope and to keep us from falling completely apart. We adopted another boy. He came to us with serious developmental delays, and we have faced many challenges with him as well, including placing him in multiple therapies for his delays. God also amazed us and our doctors with two miracle pregnancies that went to full term. Stacie and I are now the proud parents of four children—two by adoption and two by supernatural, natural means.

Amidst these blessings came more burdens. Stacie has developed fibromyalgia. She deals with bouts of soreness and pain. Our only daughter suffers from Juvenile Rheumatoid Arthritis. She was diagnosed at only eighteen months of age, and she has alternated between seasons of acute pain and remission. Our youngest son is a healthy child. Praise the Lord! He has proven, though, to be an accident waiting to happen. Our tendency is to wince when he is on the move.

Blessings and burdens—"God's good!" followed by "What's next?"

What does all this life history have to do with Asaph, the prolific writer of twelve biblical psalms, and my connection to him? It was during these times of burdens and blessings that I would consume my daily diet of the Psalms to strengthen my spirit and my walk with God. Psalm 73 especially popped off the page when I would read it. I could understand the conflict expressed by this servant of God. I could relate with his struggle to understand life's apparent inequities. I aspired to the spiritual awareness that he was able to attain. The times of conflict and confusion in my life I now call "Asaph moments." These are moments when I, like Asaph, experience secret doubts or unspoken unbelief. And I have discovered that these challenging periods of bewilderment contain within them the potential for great clarity and greater confidence in God.

In the recent past, something has happened to me that made this connection to Asaph more personal and profound. In 2009, I was diagnosed with cancer. I now have a disease that has offered me many "Asaph moments." During my treatments, I found myself turning back to Psalm 73 again and again. It is more than a psalm. It is a life saver.

Let me set the context for you, so you can understand further how this relates to me today. In 1998, Stacie and I left the youth ministry in North Carolina to plant a church in Connecticut. Through an amazing set of circumstances, God led us to start the Community Baptist Church of Branford. Our church is located in a quaint and quiet suburb of New Haven, the home of Yale University. For over ten years, the ministry made steady progress by the grace of God and in spite of my many mistakes. During that time, I was the picture of perfect health. I worked out with weights regularly and was an avid jogger.

One day, while jogging my usual three mile course, I sensed a dull pain in my back every time my feet hit the pavement. I did not think much of it at first, but as the days went by it became more frequent and discomforting. I finally had to stop jogging. I was going to the chiropractor regularly, yet the pain only progressed. I knew something was seriously wrong when my back began to lock up without warning. After a two-hour episode of this, I insisted on getting an MRI to properly identify the problem. The MRI confirmed that the pain I was feeling was indeed a serious condition. The doctors diagnosed me with a type of cancer known as Multiple Myeloma—a treatable, yet terminal form of cancer that attacks the bone structure, especially and most frequently the spine. In my case, the cancer had almost completely corrupted an entire vertebrae, and I had "holes" or lesions in others. Needless to say, the diagnosis shook me to the core and changed my world.

Following the initial diagnosis, I endured radiation, five rounds of chemotherapy, and a stem cell transplant. The side effects were as various as they were distressing: nausea, deep drowsiness, loss of appetite, loss of taste, neuropathy, and my favorite—hair loss (I've always been a "primp").

The year 2010 was definitely the most challenging year of my life. It was amazing to see God work, though. He gave me strength to stand behind the pulpit almost every Sunday. I would feel awful on Monday, terrible on Tuesday, better on Wednesday, bearable on Thursday, and then wonderful on the weekend. Of course, a pain killer pill and some steroid treatments here and there had something to do with it as well. I would tell the congregation when I was ready to preach, "Watch out, I'm a pastor on steroids!" Even though I would feel good enough to preach most Sundays, one of the greatest trials for me was the inability to give my full time and attention to the tasks of my calling.

The Psalms, which had always been a staple for me, had now become a craving. I had more time to think, read, and pray through these passionate pleas to God penned centuries ago. Psalm 73, once again, proved to be a favorite. I felt as if I could be writing the words myself. I felt as if Asaph was an unknown kindred spirit. Asaph and I are brothers in more ways than one. His inspired psalm helped me through some intensely dark moments. What I viewed initially as the curse of all curses, I now see as a blessing in disguise—a tool to draw me closer to God.

In this book, I hope to take you on a journey through this great chapter of the Bible to discover its relevant truths. I know that you will be able to identify with Asaph as I have. You will relate to his moments of confusion, envy, and secret doubts. My goal is to make this exciting exposition deep enough for you to be able to wade in with both feet, and yet, not to the depth where you feel like you are drowning in doctrine. Parts of my story will be interspersed throughout to provide experiential examples in the present context of modern Christianity.

As much as possible, I have let the Bible speak for itself. In preparation for this book, I did not comb through countless commentaries. There are no citations or endnotes. At the same time, however, there are no original thoughts here. The truths that I present are obvious and self-evident from the passage. Anyone could identify them. Since this is not a technical passage, it is possible to expound Asaph's inspired thoughts without using much of the biblical "legalese" reserved for more scholarly works. This is a devotional book. Because of this, I have added to each chapter a page of application. Included are questions useful for review, thoughtful expansion, and contemplation. These notes also make it possible for this book to be used in a group Bible study format. All Scriptural citations are from the *King James Version*—chosen for its accuracy and majestic, poetic voice. Each chapter begins with the section of the psalm that corresponds to it. Ultimately, it is the words of God themselves that are alive and able to eternally impact the heart.

My prayer for you, the reader, is that the words of the psalm and the thoughts of this book will coalesce and become cemented in your mind enough that when you face your Asaph moments you will be able to work through them to come out with greater confidence in God on the other side.

CHAPTER ONE

DISILLUSIONED

The heading of Psalm 73 tells us that this is a "*Psalm of Asaph.*" In the preface, I sought to convey my points of connection with this biblical writer. In learning more about him, I have been convinced that Asaph is a historical character with whom all believers should be familiar. Yet, I think that many hardly recognize his name. Some may not even know that he was a scriptural writer at all. If we are going to understand the contextual backdrop that defines the psalm and enhances its meaning to us, we must study all of what is recorded about Asaph's life.

Asaph is first mentioned as a temple musician in 1 Chronicles 6:39. His name is highlighted as being in a leadership position. He was a chief musician—a music director or choir director of sorts. It seems as if he and two other prominent Levitical leaders directed the musical service in the tabernacle in Jerusalem and eventually the permanent temple there. David had chosen Asaph for this position (1 Chronicles 6:31, 39). He was personally selected from among four thousand other musically gifted Levites (1 Chronicles 23:5). He must have been extremely talented to stand out in this way. He was probably a prodigy groomed from an early age for this position or something similar. His father, Berechiah, (1 Chronicles 6:39) was given the great responsibility of being a doorkeeper to the Ark of the Covenant (1 Chronicles 15:23). Asaph followed his father's footsteps in ministry leadership, carrying similar authoritative aptitude. It looks as if they even served at the same time during King David's reign (1 Chronicles 15:17 cf. 15:23). Asaph was a full-time servant of the Lord with a rich pedigree and a paternal character to go with his honored status.

Asaph was called a "singer" (1 Chronicles 15:19). He also played the cymbals (according to the same verse). In 1 Chronicles 25:6 we read about Asaph leading those who played in the orchestra. We can assume, then, that he was proficient with or at least knowledgeable in many instruments of the day. No wonder King David utilized his services in the day when the Ark was returned to Jerusalem (1 Chronicles 15:19). This was a glorious occasion that required the most glorious music possible to accentuate it. Once the Ark was settled there, Asaph was commissioned to work daily before the Ark to prepare musical selections to be performed as needed (1 Chronicles 16:37). These musical performances were designated as "prophesy" (e.g. 1 Chronicles 25:1), and Asaph later was called a "seer" (2 Chronicles 29:30). Therefore, it is no surprise to find many of his psalms included in Scripture.

There is a controversy among biblical scholars as to which of the Psalms that bear his name are truly his. Psalms 74 and 79 especially, although ascribed to Asaph, seem to be written much later. Psalm 74 describes a time when the sanctuary of the Temple was "defiled" and cast to the ground (verse 7). Psalm 79 also says that heathen invaders had defiled the temple and laid Jerusalem to ruins (verse 1). According to many scholars, this reference has to be a description of the destruction meted out against Jerusalem during the time of the Babylonian captivity. Since the Babylonian captivity occurred many generations after the death of David, the Asaph in David's day had certainly passed off the scene. The explanations most typically given for the reference to Asaph in the superscription of these psalms is that it was either a later poetic and musical writer bearing the same name who wrote them, or that one of the "sons of Asaph" wrote them—as the band of musicians who carried on his heritage used his name to define their ongoing musical guild. I have a hard time accepting these explanations due to the clear reference to Asaph in the series of Psalms from 73–83 (as if they go together being derived from one source), the mention of Jeduthun in Psalm 77 (a musical leader who also served with Asaph during King David's reign), and the similar introductory phrase "To the chief musician" used throughout the series (i.e. Psalms 75, 76, 77, 80, and 81).

Let me propose two other explanations for why Psalms 74 and 79 are ascribed to Asaph. One would be that Asaph was a prophet and was writing prophetically of destruction to come. If he was a prophet in the sense of foretelling the future, these chapters could be the record of what God revealed to him.

The other explanation is simple. In 1 Kings 14:25–28 and 2 Chronicles 12:2–12 we read about Shishak, King of Egypt, laying siege upon Jerusalem. It is said that he plundered the Temple and took away all of the "treasure of the house of the Lord" (2 Chronicles 12:9). Shishak may not have completely destroyed Jerusalem, but this invasion certainly was devastating. We are not told in the record that Shishak burned the sanctuary and broke it down, but he could have done so. We are not told that Jerusalem was in ruins, but we can imagine that an invasion such as was described would have resulted in much physical damage to the city. In fact, it is said in the account that Shishak conquered all of the fortified cities of Judah on his way to take Jerusalem (2 Chronicles 12:4). Jerusalem was spared total destruction, but it could not have escaped the kind of devastation that it would take to besiege and plunder it. If Asaph started to serve King David in his twenties, as was allowed (1 Chronicles 23:24), it is possible that he was alive during the time of this invasion during Rehoboam's reign. He would have been an old man for sure, but it is very likely that this was the case. Psalms 74 and 79 could well be Asaph's own personal notes on this tragic event and its aftermath.

If this is true, Asaph experienced many highs and lows during his time of service. He was uniquely involved in a time of spiritual revival during the time of David's early kingship. The musical ministry was one of praise, exaltation, and beauty. He also served during a time of decline and moral degradation. He saw some of this happen in David's later years. Later, he witnessed and participated in the dedication of Solomon's Temple only to see a pervasive spirit of idolatry come over the land. As I stated previously, Asaph may have even been alive to see the day when the kingdom was divided. At that time, the glorious image of the kingdom was shattered and the surrounding heathen nations took advantage of Israel's state of weakness to invade the land and plunder its riches.

It looks as if Asaph had every reason to struggle with disillusionment and doubt. Asaph had sufficient motive to question the value of his work in comparison to the overtly attractive ways of the ungodly people around him. It is a distinctly tough challenge to continue serving the Lord in times when the forms and structures around which one ministers are showing decay. Asaph faced such a challenge.

In any case, at the time of penning the words to Psalm 73, Asaph was entertaining some serious doubts. Asaph was at a point of desertion. He was at a moment of extreme consequence. How did he work through it? Asaph was experiencing some serious secret doubts…

HELP FOR YOUR SECRET DOUBTS

Questions

1. What possible highs and lows do you think Asaph experienced while serving in the temple through the different administrations?

2. How do you relate to the life of Asaph?

3. What dual promise did Jesus give us in John 16:33?

4. With the blessings of serving the Lord in ministry also come great challenges. How did the Apostle Paul describe his ministry experience in 2 Corinthians 11:23–29? What was his source of glory? (verse 30)

5. What are the three aspects of knowing Christ mentioned in Philippians 3:10? Can we ever come to this place without extreme challenge and trial?

Thought

When we surrender to serve the Lord, we can expect great privilege, blessing, and fruit for our labor. We also can expect to carry a burden. A Christian servant must count the cost in following Christ and be prepared for the realities of ministry. We must also pray daily to handle what comes our way.

CHAPTER TWO

GOD IS GOOD, BUT—

Truly God is good to Israel, even to such as are of a clean heart.—Psalm 73:1

Asaph starts his psalm with a theological affirmation: "Truly God is good to Israel, even to such as are of a clean heart." Asaph was obviously a true believer in Jehovah God. He had a convincing belief in the goodness of God, and yet he still needed further convincing as it related to the circumstances of his own life. The word "truly" could just as well be translated "surely." In modern parlance he would be saying something like, "Come on Asaph, you know this—God is good!" He was talking to himself. He was repeating personal beliefs. He was encouraging himself by repeating what he had previously understood and learned to be true in order to engender faith where faith was faltering.

All believers go through this now and then. All of us experience "Asaph moments" when faith and doubt seem to exist side by side in our minds. No one operates with 100 percent faith all of the time. All of us say to God at some time, "I believe, but help my unbelief."

Without the foundation of some level of faith in the goodness of God, a believer has no basis to trust Him further and live with any confidence during trying circumstances. If a Christian does not have the same theological conviction as Asaph, they will never be able to come to the same conclusion espoused in the later verses of Psalm 73. We must start with the belief that God is good no matter how weak that faith may be in moments of testing.

Asaph related the goodness of God to the covenant nation—Israel. Furthermore, he narrowed down the application of God's goodness to those whose hearts were cleansed of sin before God. He would never have arrived at these convictions if he did not believe in the goodness of God in general. Certainly, he was taught this as a young boy growing up in Israel. As an adult, there is no way he would have committed himself to temple service without this understanding. As we learned previously from 1 Chronicles 15:16–19, Asaph was from the priestly tribe of Levi. As such, he would have received the utmost in spiritual training. As a temple musician, certainly, many of the songs that he sang and played were praise songs celebrating the goodness of God. We saw from 1 Chronicles 16:4

and 5 that Asaph rose through the ranks to be appointed as the chief musician and worship leader. His tasks were to write songs of thanks and praise to God and to lead others in the singing and playing of the powerful testimony songs. We read of Asaph fulfilling these functions in passages like 2 Chronicles 5:1–14 and 29:20–36. He must have written and performed many songs praising the goodness of God. Writing and mouthing words is one thing; appropriating them in your emotional responses to life's trials is quite another.

The trials of life and the presence of evil are mitigating factors against a strong faith in the goodness of God. Due to these, many do not even get to first base in believing that God is good. I contend that evil and calamity do more to support the awareness of the goodness of God than they do to destroy it. The goodness of God certainly can exist independently of evil and calamity, but it is more readily recognizable because they exist. Good and evil, good or bad—can we really, as human beings, be able to fully recognize the one without the other? In fact, without goodness there would be no reference point to recognize that evil is all that evil, and the reverse can be true as well. Without calamity, goodness appears less brilliant, lacking contrast. There is no doubt that God allowed evil, but He did not originate it personally as being a direct result of His own actions. It commenced in the heart of Satan and the heart of man. God did not create evil, but He did create the conditions that allowed it to exist. Why? We can't fully know, but we can know that one result is this: the manifestation of His goodness in full form and fashion.

For any form of goodness to exist, there must be an infinite and immutable source. God is that source. Only God is eternally and essentially good. Any goodness that we are able to recognize in ourselves or outside ourselves must only be a resemblance of Him and a product of His work. When He created all things, He said of those things that they were good. Even by creating the condition for evil to exist, God expressed His goodness. Would it have been good for God to make man an automation without the ability to reason and choose? I think not. God expressed goodness by giving man a degree of freedom in which to operate and experience life. Man chose to sin. Was it not good for God to let the consequences of sin to take their full course? Was it not good for God to immediately make a way for salvation from sin? Was it not good for God to reveal Himself to man and make a way to heal his broken condition? Was it not the ultimate display of goodness for God Himself to come, experience evil in every form, and become sin—taking its full payment so that we could be saved from an eternal Hell? Truly God is good!

Romans 5:20 makes a revealing statement. It says, concerning salvation from sin, "...where sin abounded, grace did much more abound." This statement speaks to more than just salvation from sin; it tells us so much about the condition of life. It tells us that God's essential attributes are infinitely more abundant than any byproduct of the temporal effects of evil. God's goodness and the existence of evil are not equal opponents. Good and evil are not parallel, combative forces like some religious worldviews suggest.

God's goodness is immensely greater than evil by exponential degree. The calamity that we experience, which is a result of the consequence and presence of evil or sin, is far more diminished than we may think.

Think of God's creative displays of goodness. Think of the multitude of diverse stars and planetary bodies. No two are alike. Each is its own microcosm of majesty and glory. Think of earth's oceans, lakes, and rivers teeming with all forms of creatures, plants, and particles. To this point we have not begun to discover all of the marvelous manifestations of God's creative goodness on our own planet. Look at your life. Think of different aspects of goodness—actual and possible: relationships, activities, sensations, and experiences. Think of all the instruments of God's goodness. If we would just stop and consider it, we would realize that there is a plethora of ways that virtue is and can be communicated to us. What a wonderful world! What a wonderful God who made it all! Life's trials and troubles cannot compare in weight to the glory of God's goodness that shines around them and through them. It is an indictment to that depraved condition of our own spirit that we cannot recognize this truth in every moment.

Asaph had an even greater opportunity than most to recognize the goodness of God. He was an active member of the covenant people of God. All of God's creatures experience His goodness, but all do not do so to the same degree. God has reserved special gifts and blessings for those who put their trust in Him. Some see this as an indictment against God. They say, "How could a good God choose some for special blessings over others?" Some struggle with the idea of a chosen people. To understand and accept what this truth means, we must realize that God's choices are not arbitrary or capricious. He inhabits eternity (Isaiah 57:15). He sees the whole scope of human history with a panoramic view. His choices include the awareness of the responses of men. Why did God choose the nation of Israel to produce the seed of the Messiah? Why did God choose Israel to be His representatives on the earth for a time—to guard His revelation and present and portray it to the world? Among other reasons is the fact that one man, Abraham, was in a position of blessing to receive God's call and respond to it. God chose to call Abraham and to make a covenant with Him to secure the promise of the seed of salvation. Abraham chose to respond to God's call and participate in the covenant blessing. That blessing passed down to future generations until a nation was constituted for God. Asaph lived in that nation. He enjoyed the special privileges of the people of God.

At this point, it is important to recognize two facts before we mistake God's goodness for bare prejudice. First of all, God was using the nation of Israel to be a blessing to the whole world (Genesis 12:2–3). Also, just being in the covenant nation did not secure one's salvation from sin or their full experience of God's covenant blessing (Jeremiah 4:1–4). God is a just God as much as He is a good God. In fact, His justice is good. So without a clean heart toward God, and with the presence of regarded sin, one would actually be in the path of God's displeasure and discipline as opposed to being in the path of

His choicest blessings. Asaph got it right when he said, "Truly God is good to Israel, even to such as are of a clean heart."

Asaph knew his theological facts. He had his catechism down. His theological affirmation was the expression of a strong religious heritage. I can relate. I was reared in a covenant family as well—a New Covenant family. Let me explain. My father, Joe Zacharias, came to know Christ as his personal Saviour when he was a young man in the military, around the time of the Korean War. Not long after, my dad answered the call to full-time ministry and began training to be a pastor. He attended Bethel College in St. Paul and Trinity Evangelical Divinity School in Chicago. For over thirty-five years he pastored different churches in Michigan. He pastored an Evangelical Free church, a Bible church, and an independent Baptist church. I grew up in a home where the New Covenant blessing of my father's salvation and ministry produced many privileges for me. I heard the gospel frequently. I received solid biblical training. I came to receive Christ as my Savior at nine years old and continued to grow as I learned more about Him in church. My life was centered around the church. I began singing in church at age five. I served the Lord with my father and learned under his teaching. I memorized countless Scripture passages in Sunday school, Christian school, Vacation Bible School, and summer camp. I knew the biblical facts about God. I believed them. But life was somewhat easy then.

Later on, when life became extremely challenging, I began to sense persistent doubts within my spirit. My thoughts would go like this, “I know what is true but…” “I know what I believe but…” “I know God is good but…” Like Asaph, even in the ministry while leading others, these doubts would surface in my mind from time to time. Each challenge I faced became an opportunity to work through the confusion and cooperate with God in order to shore up my confidence in Him. But, like Asaph, confidence did not succeed without overcoming the obstacle of many “buts,” “whys,” and “what-ifs.”

HELP FOR YOUR SECRET DOUBTS

Questions

1. In Psalm 27:13, what comes first, believing or seeing, as it relates to the goodness of God?

2. Do you think it is possible to believe in the goodness of God without always perceiving it? How so?

3. According to Psalm 27:13, what happens when we don't believe in the goodness of God?

4. What are men told to do in Psalm 107:8, 15, 21, and 31? Is it implied in this psalm that we generally do or do not?

5. David says in Psalm 144:2 that God is his goodness. What do you think that means?

Thought

Without an awareness of the goodness of God, we will never survive the trials of life. We must realize that this awareness comes by faith and through God's Word, not through our circumstances only. Also, we must see our relationship with God as the ultimate source of goodness for us. When we miss this truth, we are left looking for goodness in a cursed place. This can lead to emotional turmoil, as we will see.

CHAPTER THREE

AM I THE EXCEPTION?

But as for me, my feet were almost gone; my steps had well-nigh slipped.—Psalm 73:2

We use a little conjunction with God all the time. It is a conjunction of excuse: "I know You are calling me to do this, *but*…." It is a conjunction of defiance: "I know what Your Word says, *but*…." It is also a conjunction of confusion and doubt: "I'm sure You are good, *but*…." I think that Asaph's usage here reflects the latter, although it could be that he was expressing his lack of purity at heart. In that case, the "*but*" would relate to a contrast between his life and those with clean hearts. To me, it seems more natural to interpret this verse in the psalm as an expression of doubt concerning God's personal goodness in light of his current circumstances. In this case, the "*but*" would be a note of confusion. This matches the greater context as he sees the apparent success of the wicked. Either way, he was saying that his life was lacking some aspect of the awareness of God's blessing. He was experiencing a slouching sense of confidence in God. He felt as if he were the exception to the general rule that God is good to His people.

In verse 2, Asaph is bemoaning the fact that he was on the brink of utter despair and possible defection from the work of God. He was stumbling. He was slipping. He was backsliding.

His condition is easy to understand since the ministry is the source of not only much pleasure but also much frustration. The life of serving God is fraught with countless conflicts. As Paul said, "A great door…is opened unto me and there are many adversaries" (1 Corinthians 16:9). There are many detours on the road of full-time ministry. There are many dangers. The way is strewn with many casualties. John Mark called it quits for a season (Acts 12:25 cf., 13:13). Demas couldn't take it (2 Timothy 4:10). Many ministers of God have done the same down through the centuries. I have witnessed much ministry defection firsthand. Three of my closest mentors in the ministry stepped down due to moral failure. I'm certain that each moral lapse did not occur in a vacuum. Each one of these men had to experience some great spiritual conflict in the years preceding their acts of shameful sin. I met a seasoned pastor who expressed his thoughts on this subject this way: "When I was a young pastor, I admired the guys who could really preach. As a middle-aged pastor, I appreciated my colleagues who could administer a large congregation and many other ministries. Now that I am an older pastor, I just admire the older guys who, like me, are still in the ministry."

I wonder how many full-time ministers of God have found themselves on the brink like Asaph? I've even heard some pastors say in jest, "Every Monday, I entertain the thought of quitting." That expression may be an exaggeration, but it represents a reality with which all those who serve the Lord can relate. It is easy to become weary in well doing. It is common to consider greener grasses and more pleasant places. I'll admit it. I've been there.

My ministry has been one of the most exciting and fulfilling endeavors of my life. And yet, there have been countless occasions that have been the cause for confusion and doubt. I can say that there have been many times when "my steps had well-nigh slipped."

The first occasion that comes to mind was a time soon after my wife's first miscarriage. We had experienced nearly three years of infertility and countless tests, so when we announced her pregnancy to our families and the church, everyone was extremely excited for us. It was a very low moment when we realized that it was not meant to be. That was followed by many low moments as we had to constantly hear each member of the church tell us how sorry they were for us.

After that time, I was shocked with myself. I actually considered walking away from the ministry. Also, the youth ministry in which we were involved had proven to produce little fruit to that point. Of course, what can you expect when you have been at it for such a short time? We only served at that church for seven years total. Stacie's first miscarriage came at the outset of our ministry there. Fruit takes time. Any harvest is the result of countless hours of sowing and cultivating. We realize that now. We were in a hurry to see a harvest then. I remember saying to myself, "Why am I doing this? Where are the blessings I expected? Maybe I should have continued my training to be an accountant."

When we started the church in Branford, every Sunday was full of challenges. During those first years of ministry, we never knew what would happen during any given service. We met in the conference room of a rundown hotel. During one Easter service, we heard a toilet flush on the floor above us. This was soon followed by water cascading down on a row of visitors. (Do you think any of those visitors returned?) Before a Christmas service, a man entered the building loudly announcing that he was Jesus. This man became so belligerent in the hallway that two of our ushers had to forcibly remove him. Afterwards, they came to tell me what had happened. I said with a smirk, "Great, you just kicked Jesus out of our Christmas service!"

One of the lowest moments for me came when our highest-attended Sunday was followed by our lowest. This brought to my mind the realization that this thing was hanging on by a thread. We were only one Sunday away from extinction. I called a seasoned church planter that I respected. He gave me some advice that kept me from throwing in the towel. He said, "Don't judge the success of your ministry by how many attend on any given Sunday." From that point on, we did not record our attendance in the bulletin. To this day, I do not know the exact count on any Sunday. This prevents me from experiencing the extremes of elation and depression that I derive from "the numbers."

If I have learned anything over the years, it is this: Many of God's greatest blessings come down the road. Some are reserved for Heaven. Satan's way is easy up front, and the hard stuff comes later. God's way is hard at first, but the blessings come by and by. Many Christians do not persevere in service long enough to receive the benefits.

I'm sure that Asaph knew these realities in God's economy. By the time he had written this psalm, he must have notched many years of ministry on his belt; and yet, still he struggled with confusion, disappointment, covetousness, and envy. In the following verses, he talks like a little boy who is doing his homework in his room while his neighborhood buddies are having a snowball fight outside. He sounds as if his face is pressed up against the window as he thinks to himself, "Why am I here when I could be out there with them?"

You do not have to be in full-time ministry to have experienced these invasive thoughts. Of course, all of us should be full-time servants of God in the truest sense, but you know what I mean by full-time ministry. That's the person who gets paid for serving the Lord. I think that the Christian who doesn't get paid—in an earthly, monetary sense—for serving the Lord is even more susceptible to serious, secret doubts. The tangible benefits for their labor are reserved in Heaven.

It's hard to work for much less down here. Could that be why so many Christian servants don't stay so long in service? Show me the Sunday School teacher that has logged twenty-five years or more of service. Show me the deacon whose duty has spanned the decades. That kind of faithfulness seems rare. It seems as if one of the consistent character traits of Christian workers is inconsistency. Many struggle with staying at it. It is not surprising to see some who have served in the past now sitting on the sidelines and taking a break. Some are faithful in the church but "checked out" in their seat. Others are out of church as much as they are in it. Those who actively serve in the trenches—watching others come and go in the meantime—can easily become embittered like Asaph. There may be more people going through the motions of ministry than we think.

Let's face it—the Christian life is not easy. For sure, God will partner with us to lighten the load, but if we pull out of the yoke, we'll have a hard row to plough. Since no Christian operates with 100 percent faithfulness, there are sure to come times of consternation. We begin to say: "I know God is good, but..." "Truly God is great and all; but as for me, I'm on the ropes and going down for the count."

HELP FOR YOUR SECRET DOUBTS

Questions

(Read Psalm 26 and refer to the noted verses for these questions)

1. According to verse 1, what do we have to do so that we do not slide or slip on the path of life?

2. In verse 4, what corresponding activity will also keep us from sliding?

3. What discipline is being described in verse 6? How will this keep us from slipping?

4. What is one of the main goals of the believer according to verse 7? Do you think this contributes to stability in our lives?

5. According to verses 8 and 12, where is one of the best places to be to engender consistency in our lives?

Thought

The Christian walk is a precarious one if we are not firmly committed to the Word of God, prayer, confession, and the fellowship of the believers. We are so prone to falling. Like gravity, our sin nature is pulling us down to the earth. It takes the strength of God to stay standing and keep walking. That strength is available—especially when we are about to slip.

CHAPTER FOUR

WHY THEM?

For I was envious at the foolish, when I saw the prosperity of the wicked. For there are no bands in their death: but their strength is firm. They are not in trouble as other men; neither are they plagued like other men. Therefore pride compasseth them about as a chain; violence covereth them as a garment. Their eyes stand out with fatness: they have more than heart could wish. They are corrupt and speak wickedly concerning oppression: they speak loftily. They set their mouth against the heavens, and their tongue walketh throughout the earth.—PSALM 73:3–9

In verse three of the psalm, Asaph says that he "was envious at the foolish" when he "saw the prosperity of the wicked." Envy is a serious and subtle sin. It is a close kin to covetousness. In fact, envy and covetousness are sister sins. When, in times of trouble, we say "Why me?", it is so easy for us to, in turn, look at the apparent prosperity of others and say, "Why them?" When we look at the condition of others with an inordinate longing for what they have or who they are, we are committing a gross transgression against God. We are, in a sense, saying that God's provision for us is not sufficient. It is not good enough. This is what happens when we are struggling with our belief in the goodness of God. Envy is always there seeking entrance into the door of our hearts. And it is impossible to envy others without coveting who they are or what they have. That's why Asaph said it was the seeming prosperity of the wicked that set his heart to envy. Although this may seem like an innocuous inward sin, it is not. We must remember that it is from the heart that the issues of our lives flow (Proverbs 4:23). Envy and covetousness are sinful attitudes that produce sinful actions.

I find it interesting that the Ten Commandments begin and end with some form of these sins. The first commandment says to place no other gods above God (Exodus 20:3). In the Bible, the general reference of the word "gods" is to some man-made form of deity. It also is used to refer to some earthly object that takes priority over the One True God. Philippians 3:19 describes those who are antagonistic to the cross of Jesus Christ. It says that their "...god is their belly" and "...they mind earthly things." Idolatry can be a form of covetousness as we look to the things of this earth for satisfaction. Idolatry can involve envy as we direct our deepest desires to those things that are not our own. Also, the final command of the Ten Commandments is against covetousness in particular. Envy is implied as we are told not to covet our neighbor's possessions. How could one do that without envy? The two go together. They are both at the top of the list of consequential sins.

I also find it interesting that covetousness is well placed in the list of publicly shameful sins that should be disciplined in the church (1 Corinthians 5:11). According to this passage, Christians should not enjoy close fellowship with unrepentant offenders, and it seems as if these offenders should also be removed from the church. We must identify those involved, approach them in love, and confront them with the goal of true conviction and change. Once confronted, if the offender does not repent and make repairs, the church is told not to "keep company" with him or her (verse 11). Paul tells the church to put away from them any "wicked person" in this regard (verse 13). In the list of these offensive sins, the sin of covetousness is mentioned with fornication, drunkenness, extortion, railing, and idolatry. I can see how these are readily recognizable and obviously identified. How could this be said of covetousness? When is the last time you were in a church that disciplined one of its members concerning covetousness?

As a pastor who wants to follow these biblical injunctions about church life, I have thought long and hard about this. I would say that covetousness is listed as a disciplinary sin because it naturally works itself out to affect a believer's commitment to the church and its service. A covetous Christian would care more about making money than being faithful to church. A covetous Christian would care more about "keeping up with the Joneses" than serving Jesus. A covetous Christian is worldly, wanton, and wayward. Sometimes, after much cajoling, the only recourse left that will wake such a one out of their stupor is local church censure. If they feel that they can keep one little toe in the church while living a life characterized by covetousness—if they feel that they can be covetous with impunity—what reason do they have to change?

Asaph's envy could have easily worked its way out in his life to the place where he became disqualified for public ministry. Envious thoughts are destructive. It is essentially foolish to envy the foolish. It is essentially wicked to envy the wicked.

In Asaph's case, as with anyone else, his envy caused him to see the condition of others in a skewed manner. He began to look at the foolish and the wicked with a selective eye, only observing the apparent advantages and benefits of their lives and lifestyles. He looked past the bad and saw the good. He looked past the problems to see the profit. He looked past the rule and saw the exception. He said, "The wicked have it good!" The only way he could make this observation was to set his sights on only those who outwardly seemed so successful, healthy, wealthy, and care-free.

In verse 3, Asaph sees the wicked as prosperous. In verse 4, Asaph bemoans the fact that many wicked and foolish people seem to be living stronger lives and dying more peaceful deaths than the righteous servants of God. Of course, this viewpoint is not always true, but when we are struggling, like Asaph, we tend to see it that way. If we are not careful, we may even think that as faithful servants of God, we *deserve* good health and monetary ease. I know that the Bible does not teach this perspective, and yet, I have entertained the invading thought, "Why do I have cancer when I have been faithful to serve the Lord?" or "Why do I have financial struggles after all I have given to the Lord's work?"

I suspect that God's people have always battled these thoughts. It doesn't help either to hear the constant tribe of "health and wealth" preachers who tell us that we should never accept sickness and financial deprivation. Honestly, I do not understand how anyone who claims to know and teach the Bible could justify these doctrines. How do they explain Job? How do they explain the privation of Jesus (Matthew 8:20, Luke 9:58)? How do they explain the fact that God told Paul to keep his infirmity (2 Corinthians 12:7–12)? How do they explain the sickness of Epaphroditis and Trophimus? Both of these men were sick while faithfully serving the Lord (Philippians 2:25–30, 2 Timothy 4:20). How do they explain the fact that Paul told Timothy to expect infirmity often (1 Timothy 5:23)? How do they explain the "others" mentioned in Hebrews 11:36–39 who endured persecution, torture, torment, and cruel deaths all in the name of the Lord? Certainly God can deliver us from tribulation. Certainly God can heal the sick. Certainly He has made provision through prayer (James 5:14–16). That does not mean that we can expect healing and deliverance in every case. If that were true, we would never die.

What we can expect is that sickness and death are a part of life. We can also expect that some will be healthier than others. This is as true among the unbelieving wicked as it is among the people of God. We can also expect that if we love God and are called according to His purpose, anything we endure will eventually work out for good (Romans 8:28).

Asaph was not seeing straight. In verse 5 he says that some foolish and wicked men seem to have no trouble at all. What a blinded perspective! The problem is that we usually see only puncticular or moment-in-time conditions. We are not able to view the whole context of a person's life. We are also not able to view the turmoil inside their soul.

I think what really bothered Asaph was that these people were wicked and, as such, did not deserve any pleasure and profit in life. In verse 6, he says that they are prideful and violent. In verses 8 and 9, he says that they are corrupt and curse God and men. And yet for all that, he says in verse 7, "they have more than heart could wish."

Inherent in all of these thoughts written by Asaph is the implied expectation of earthly blessings. He was secretly wondering, "When is my service for God going to pay?" Besides not experiencing blessing, he was being plagued and chastened every day (verse 14).

Doesn't God promise blessings to all those who serve Him? Yes, but blessings come in many forms, and God determines when they come and in which form they arrive. Blessings can be spiritual, relational, financial, mental, physical, earthly, and eternal. When, in envy, we set our eyes on the people of this world, we miss the varieties of blessing that God gives in a trial. One of the greatest blessings is contentment—finding our portion in Him alone and not being so emotionally affected by the ups and downs of life. Asaph lost that sublime sense for a moment, and he is not alone.

HELP FOR YOUR SECRET DOUBTS

Questions

1. What does Hebrews 13:5 imply is the opposite of covetousness?

2. What is the basis for that condition found in the same verse?

3. When Romans 8:28 says that "all things work together for good," what does that mean? What qualifiers define that phrase? What is the good purpose in our lives that God is working out according to the next verse (verse 29)?

4. Philippians 4:13 describes the confidence of the Apostle Paul. According to the previous context in verses 10–12, what are the "all things" referred to in verse 13 that Paul believed he could do in Christ?

5. How prevalent are the sins of envy and covetousness in your life? According to Philippians 4:10–12, what does it take to conquer these sins?

Thought

Envy and covetousness are scourges to the Christian. They lead to many other sins and wayward ways. By God's grace, we can learn to be content. Contentment takes time to attain, but it is possible. Christ exemplified perfect contentment in His life. There was no hint of envy in Him. He will be our teacher if we let Him.

CHAPTER FIVE

DOES GOD REALLY KNOW?

Therefore his people return hither: and waters of a full cup are wrung out to them. And they say, How doth God know? And is there knowledge in the Most High?—PSALM 73:10–11

Verse 10 of Asaph's psalm is a great example of how commentaries can sometimes prove to be contradictory and confusing in interpreting the Bible. Each commentator you may read concerning this verse will have a different take on it. Let me suggest my own dime store exposition (and either add to or clear up the confusion—you decide).

First, the phrase, "Therefore his people return hither" certainly refers to the people of God. The pronoun "his" cannot refer to the ungodly wicked since, in the previous context, they are referred to in the plural forms of "their" and "they." It must refer back to "God" from verse 1. That would make "his people" none other than the covenant nation of Israel.

Second, when it says that they "return hither" (i.e. return here or to this place), the suggestion is that Asaph is saying that God's people come at some time to where He is. Asaph would seem to be referring to his place of employment—the Temple.

Finally, the phrase "and waters of a full cup are wrung out to them" implies that while the wicked around them are prosperous, the people of God are made to drink the bitter cup of trial and tragedy.

This is where it gets even more confusing. The next verse says, "And they say, How doth God know? And is there knowledge in the Most High?" Does the word "they" refer to God's people or back to the ungodly of verse 9 who have "set their mouth against the heavens"? Is it God's people who are questioning the knowledge of God or the wicked ones who walk the earth? I tend to believe that this refers to God's people. If what I believe is true, then Asaph is accounting for the prevailing sense of doubt among the people of God. They come to the Temple for worship at times with the untoward mixture of devotion and discouragement. From his thoughts in verses 13 and 14, we could conclude that he felt this conflict as well. God's people have always struggled with these types of thoughts. And if the ungodly chime in with the refrain "Where is your God?" it makes matters even worse.

In Job 22:13, Eliphaz accuses Job of such thoughts. He says to Job, "And thou sayest, How doth God know? Can he judge through the dark cloud?" Whether true or not, as it relates to Job, Eliphaz accounts for a common sentiment among God's people. We all say to ourselves at some time or another, "Does God really know what I am going through? Can God really see through the dark clouds above me?" Following those thoughts is the corresponding thought: "If He can, why doesn't He do something?"

This kind of doubting among God's people is more emotional in nature than it is intellectual. For sure, there is such a thing as intellectual doubt. Intellectual uncertainty is based on our response to reason, facts, or the lack thereof. We may read a passage in the Bible concerning something supernatural or transcendent and say, "I cannot reason my way through this; I wonder if it is true." Only the Holy Spirit can infuse in us the confidence that is needed to believe the bare and sometimes incomprehensible words of God.

I propose, however, that much of our doubting is not intellectual in nature—it is our underlying feelings that are at the source of uncertainty. Our doubts come from how we *feel* about our circumstances, and they are based on how we interpret them. The prominent issue is not facts but our emotional responses to what is happening in our lives. These are feelings that assault our beliefs and convictions. These are imaginations that arrest our ability to reason.

Since this kind of doubting is essentially emotional, it relates to and results in other emotional responses such as fear and anxiety. Fear concerns that which is real or actual—that which we are facing. Anxiety concerns that which is possible—

that which may come down the road. Both of these can emanate from a lack of faith in God.

Psychologists talk about "intrusive thoughts." These are thoughts which take over our minds and strongly influence our emotional state. The Bible describes these kinds of doubts as imaginations that exalt themselves against the knowledge of God (2 Corinthians 10:5). They proceed from our own faithless hearts. They subsist in our spirits as rehearsed by a whispering world of evil spirits. They can and must be cast out.

The solution is not to empty our minds of all else (as if there were such a thing as "non-thinking" as some New Age philosophers suggest). The Bible remedy for the believer is to proactively pray for God's grace to take away these thoughts so that they do not linger and languish in our minds.

An example of emotional doubt is found in the life of John the Baptist. In John 1:29, when John first sees Jesus, he says with confidence, "Behold the Lamb of God, which taketh away the sin of the world." Later in Matthew 11:2–3, we read where John sent some of his disciples to question Jesus. They asked, "Are you the real Messiah or are we looking for someone else?" (my paraphrase). What changed in John's life that contributed to this shift to diminishing confidence? In the latter passage, John was in prison. I propose that the source of his doubts was his emotional reaction to his circumstances. It was the pain of prison and the fear of death. His circumstances were contrary to his beliefs. He was saying to himself, "If Jesus is really the Messiah, then why is this happening to me, His faithful servant?"

Peter experienced emotional doubt when he walked on the water. In Matthew 14:22–33, we read this famous account. For sure, Peter should get some credit here for having enough faith to get off the boat and take those initial steps out onto the raging sea. Verse 29 says, "...he walked on the water." Amazing! But verse 30 records a sudden change in conviction. When the winds turned "boisterous," he gave in to fear and began to sink. In grace, Jesus put forth His hand and pulled Peter from danger. Then Jesus said, "O thou of little faith, wherefore didst thou doubt?" What changed for Peter that caused him to so quickly reconsider his previously held confidence? His view of the circumstances changed. It changed as he focused on the wind, the waves, and the weather.

What happened to John the Baptist and Peter happens to all of us at times. Our doubts reflect emotional changes first and foremost. These emotional doubts are dangerous. Uncertainty can easily lead to a pervasive sense of skepticism. We can become skeptical about all of God's promised blessings. Skepticism leads to unbelief and disbelief. Unbelief is more of a natural reaction; disbelief is more of a deliberate and intentional action. These thoughts are the seeds for direct disobedience and rebellion toward God. Living for God requires faith in the supremacy of His sovereignty and a confidence in His will. Without these we are prone to do our own thing; and that way charts the course to many pitfalls in life.

Psalms 42 and 43 give us a pattern and prescription for conquering these doubts. Most scholars agree that these psalms were meant as a continuing thought. They go together. In them, the psalmist displays a striking fluctuation in mood. In verse 1 of Psalm 42, he expresses longing for God—as a deer panting for water, his heart is panting for God. In verse 3, he expresses sorrow as he weeps incessantly. His grief compounds as people say to him in his struggle, "Where is thy God?" In verse 4, he expresses painful reflection, and he thinks of better days. In verse 6, he professes a sense of depression concerning his circumstances. He says, "O my God, my soul is cast down within me..." In verse 9, he conveys confusion as he asks God, "Why hast thou forgotten me?" And yet, through all this, he interjects glimpses of hope and faith. Chapter 43 ends with a note of confidence. With all that was going on in his mind, how was he able to get there? How was he able to find any measure of faith?

First, it is evident that he recognized his wrong feelings and doubts. Throughout, he said to himself, "Why are you cast down?" or "Why are you feeling this way?" Implied is the sense that he knew that these thoughts were aberrant and unacceptable. This is the first key to victory. When we begin to accept our doubtful thoughts, and indulge in them to the degree where we consider them tolerable, we are in trouble. When we reject them out of hand, there is hope to cast them out.

Second, the psalmist talked to himself with the truth. He repeated to himself statements of positive affirmation. He said, "God is my help and the health of my countenance" (42:5, 11; 43:5). Like him, we must use the Scriptures and the truths contained in them to combat our evil thoughts. Finally, he prayed for more light and truth to lead him to an attitude of joy and hope (43:3–4).

Sounds too simple to work: recognize wrong thoughts, rehearse God's truth, and request more light from God; but if we do these three things, we will find that our doubts will diminish and even disappear. Asaph did just that, as we will see. But first, he admits to more uncertainty and confusion.

HELP FOR YOUR SECRET DOUBTS

Questions

Read John 20:24–31 and refer to the noted verses for these questions.

1. What was the nature of Thomas's doubts—intellectual, emotional, or both? Why?

2. What source of evidence did not persuade Thomas according to verse 25?

3. What form of proof finally persuaded Thomas?

4. Is there a possibility that, in this lifetime, we will receive the same evidence that Thomas received? If not, does that mean that we have no evidence to fuel our faith? What other evidence do we have on which to operate? What is one source of evidence mentioned in verse 31?

5. What does God say about those who believe in God while not seeing Him (verse 29)?

Thought

As Christians, we must not accept any form of doubt in our lives. Just because doubts are natural does not make them acceptable. Faith comes by the Word (Romans 10:17); it is by this means that God can give us the faith necessary to avoid evil and seek His will for our lives.

CHAPTER SIX

WHAT'S THE USE?

Behold, these are the ungodly, who prosper in the world; they increase in riches. Verily, I have cleansed my heart in vain, and washed my hands in innocency. For all the day long have I been plagued and chastened every morning.
—Psalm 73:12–14

Verses 12–14 of Psalm 73 express an extremely low point in the progression of Asaph's doubtful thoughts. In verse 12, he sums up his previous skewed observations by saying that the ungodly not only seem to prosper, but their prosperity increases as time goes by. The rich are getting richer. The rich are having "champagne wishes and caviar dreams" (as Robin Leach would say), while the righteous are struggling to survive.

Asaph saw that things were getting better for the ungodly, while things were seemingly getting worse for him. In verse 14, he complains, "For all the day long have I been plagued, and chastened every morning." What a sad sentiment! It is because of this condition, as compared to the ungodly rich, that Asaph is led to believe that he was righteous in vain and naïve for seeking to live right. In verse 13, he essentially says, "What's the use?"

I doubt any Christian experiences complete victory over these kinds of invasive thoughts. Keeping a clean heart is a trying endeavor. Without the help of God, none of us would have the moral constitution sufficient for the task. It is easy to become disappointed. All, at some time, wonder if throwing in the towel is a better option. I'm sure that every Christian, at least at some point, entertains the tempting thought of throwing up their hands and quitting the righteous life. The way of the world looks easier. It is filled with ecstasy and fleshly enjoyment. "What is the benefit to holiness?" we ask, "when there is so much immediate pleasure to be gained by hedonism?" Holiness is so hard.

Fleshly living is so much fun. Without any perceived benefit in holiness, we can quickly lose our motivation for it.

Here's what we must keep in mind: holiness is an exponential proposition. In other words, the tangible fruits are not always immediate. They come down the road. The benefits of holiness accrue and increasingly compound until they come to full light and fruition in the eternal state. One must have an eye to eternity to see the benefits of holiness.

Fleshy pursuits produce only immediate pleasures. These pleasures are strong, for sure, but they disappear as quickly as they come. They diminish over time, leaving deep cravings in their place; and the deeper the craving, the more diminished the capacity for enjoyment. It takes more to feel good. It takes less to feel bad. Holiness is always better than hedonism. It's just hard to see it when all you are using is your physical eyes.

Moses was able to figure this out. Hebrews 11:25 says that he chose "rather to suffer affliction with the people of God, than to enjoy the pleasures of sin for a season." This decision manifested a great degree of faith. That's why it is included in the great faith chapter of the Bible. As Christians, we need faith to choose and refuse, to denounce and confess, to relinquish this evil world's lustful pleasures and embrace the will of God no matter the cost at the time.

Moses did that by being willing to give up the prestige, name recognition, power, and fame associated with being called the son of Pharaoh's daughter. I don't know if most of us can even relate to or imagine the degree of privilege that came from such a standing in society. He gave up the pleasures that accompanied this position. Certainly, people waited on him to meet his every need. Moses had an array of sinful pleasures always available to him—ready at his beck and call.

Let's face it: many of us would struggle with leaving all that behind. We are naturally hedonistic. We all love sinful pleasures. They are tantalizing and stimulating, but they are also short-lived. They are fleeting. Those who live for pleasure are destined for a life of vanity. Observe this excerpt from

Job 20:4–7: "Knowest thou not this of old, since man was placed upon the earth, that the triumphing of the wicked is short, and the joy of the hypocrite is but for a moment? Though his excellency mount up to the heavens, and his head reach unto the clouds; yet he shall perish for ever like his own dung: they which have seen him shall say, Where is he?" Moses knew this. Asaph had forgotten for a time.

Verse 26 of Hebrews 11 goes on to say that Moses esteemed "the reproach of Christ greater riches than the treasures of Egypt: for he had respect unto the recompense of reward." Astounding! He gave up riches and chose reproach. He chose to suffer affliction. He chose the "reproach of Christ." (This is an interesting phrase since Christ had not yet been born. It goes to show that the Old Testament believers looking forward to the Messiah were actually living for Jesus.)

The New Testament tells us, "all that will live godly in Christ Jesus shall suffer persecution" (2 Timothy 3:12). You might be saying, "Where do I sign up?" More likely you're saying, "Really, who would do this?" Only those who know what Moses knew. Moses chose reproach for Christ because he had great respect for the recompense of the reward for righteous living. He had anticipation for God's eventual blessing in this life and the life to come.

When you or I say, "What's the use?" we are forgetting God's amazing benefit package for righteousness in Him. Paul said in 2 Corinthians 4:17, "For our light affliction, which is but for a moment, worketh (accomplishes, performs, or produces) for us a far more exceeding and eternal weight of glory." What a contrast. Our affliction is light. Our tangible reward in Heaven is heavy. Our affliction is for a moment. Our reward in Heaven is eternal.

In Matthew 19:27, Peter said to Jesus, "...Behold, we have forsaken all and followed thee; what shall we have therefore?" Jesus responded with a fascinating answer. He did not say to Peter, "What kind of question is that?" or "How selfish can you be? You should sacrifice for sacrifice sake." Instead Jesus said this (verses 28 and 29): "...Verily I say unto you, That ye which have followed me, in the regeneration when the Son of man shall sit in the throne of his glory, ye also shall sit upon twelve thrones, judging the twelve tribes of Israel. And every one that hath forsaken houses, or brethren, or sisters, or father, or mother, or wife, or children, or lands, for my name's sake, shall receive an hundredfold, and shall inherit everlasting life." Wow! What an answer! It says that God gives more than He takes. Whatever we give up will be replaced with something more valuable, solid, and substantial in the eternal kingdom of Christ.

In the end, no one loses who chooses to take up his cross to follow Jesus. When affliction comes, we need to remember this. We should not look to the world with longing eyes. If we are being plagued, it is for a purpose. If we are being chastened, it is for our good. When we say, "What's the use of living right?" we are displaying a dangerous lack of discernment that will lead us to a major detour on our course for Christ.

Asaph was about as low as a believer can go. I have been there. I've plunged the depths into the pit of self-pity. I said,

"What's the use?" For me, there was a season of one trial after another. Cancer seemed like a plague greater than I could bear. In my weak moments, I thought to myself, "So this is how a life of ministry pays off?! This is not what I signed up for." These are vain thoughts. They take us to no good place.

One of the most challenging parts of the ministry is to hide your negative thoughts while you continue to serve God and others. Many in the ministry become masters of repression. They know how to look happy on the outside while a cauldron of distress is brewing within. In the next verses, Asaph accounts for his depressive repression and how he was able to hold it all in.

HELP FOR YOUR SECRET DOUBTS

Questions

1. What Bible character essentially said, "What's the use?" in 1 Kings 19:4–5? What brought him to this place (verses 1–3)?

2. Read 2 Corinthians 4:8. Do you think that there is a difference between disappointment and discouragement? Is there a difference between depression and despair? What are the differences?

3. Does God provide resources to defeat bitterness and depression in our lives? What does Hebrews 12:12–15 say about this? What are the steps to victory in this passage?

4. According to Hebrews 12:15, what are we missing if we are struggling with depressive thoughts?

5. What is God's formula for productive thinking found in Philippians 4:6–9? Where can we procure these kinds of thoughts?

Thought

We cross the line from simple discouragement to despair when we respond sinfully to life's circumstances. Questioning

God turns into making indictments against Him. Sadness can quickly turn to self-pity. God's grace and His truth can keep us from crossing that line.

CHAPTER SEVEN

SECRET DOUBTS

If I say, I will speak thus; behold, I should offend against the generation of thy children. When I thought to know this, it was too painful for me.—Psalm 73:15–16

Asaph says something in verse 15 to which every full-time servant of the Lord can relate. He says that he is hesitant to speak what he is thinking lest he would offend another child of God. He could not bring himself to express his secret doubts. In verse 16, he explains that he was stuck between two painful choices: expressing his doubts would risk bringing a discouraging influence upon the people of God—a consequence beyond what he could bear. Yet, keeping the thoughts inside was unbearable as well. One way or another, given his continual work among the people of God, these thoughts were sure to come out. He was at a point of such conflict.

I wonder how many full-time pastors, missionaries, and teachers struggle with secret doubts. I would dare say that they all do at one time or another. Many wrestle with their own lack of confidence, even while teaching others concerning their need of greater confidence in God. Some would call that the height of hypocrisy. I call it human nature.

Thomas struggled with doubts, and he had the privilege of seeing the supernatural works of Jesus firsthand. Peter, in utter discouragement, went back to fishing after the death of Jesus. His dogma soon turned to doubt in a matter of hours when he was faced with circumstances that seemed to work out in a way counter to his previous conviction. Eve doubted God. Abraham and Sarah doubted God. Gideon doubted God. Even Elijah doubted God. If these great stalwarts of the faith dealt with such thoughts, can any Christian be immune to the same?

Those who serve the Lord in ministry have an added burden here. They are responsible for their influence and leadership to the people of God. They cannot go around blurting out doubts. Their doubts usually stay hidden—suppressed. Yet, even when not expressed verbally, these doubts tend to work themselves out. Those unexpressed thoughts in the minds of God's choice servants can fester, causing an eventual breakdown that will manifest itself in how they minister. It is unavoidable. Doubts have to be dealt with. If not, defection from service becomes the only remedy to escape insanity. Why do so many leave full-time ministries? I believe one of the main reasons is that they doubt the goodness of God.

Picture a young, somewhat naïve pastor. He enters the ministry with the highest ideals—with great plans and purposes. Sure, he knows life will not be easy, but amidst the challenges, he sees a life of blessing and fruitfulness. He sees health and harmony with God's people in his future. That image can easily be shattered by unforeseen sources of affliction. The mature, seasoned pastor knows the reality of ministry. He can say with the Apostle Paul, "...a great door...is opened unto me, and there are many adversaries" (1 Corinthians 16:9). A young servant may not know this. He does not have the experience to prepare for what's ahead. Because of this, many do not make it for long in the ministry. They are soon down for the count. What a shame! What a tragedy! What a crime! Most of the time, the culprit is doubtful thoughts fueled by the willing accessories of demonic spirits who repeat them.

Asaph was on the edge. His inner turmoil was so palpable he could hardly contain it. I know the feeling. I'll never forget the low times I experienced in dealing with my oldest adopted son. I said to myself, "We adopted this boy with the best intentions. Why is God allowing this to happen? Why is this not turning out for good?" It seemed as if I was leading two lives—my home life, and my church life. When things at church were going well, my home life was in turmoil. When I would experience a short reprieve from trouble at home, then a problem would surface at church. It was always something.

I remember driving in my car one day in a mental fog. I turned on a song about Heaven and started to cry. I felt as if I wanted to just drive my car over the bridge and end it all. Surely God would excuse my premature arrival. At least I still believed in Heaven. My confidence in the goodness of God on earth was at an all-time low. Obviously, I did not follow through with those destructive thoughts. In fact, not only did I not drive over the bridge, but the following Sunday there I was, in my place, preaching the virtues of God and His will. Don't be shocked. Every pastor who has served any length of time knows exactly what I am talking about—even your pastor. Just ask him if he has ever had secret doubts. Look at yourself. If you have been saved long enough to experience a significant season of adversity since you met the Lord, you have to admit there have been times when you cried out to God, "I believe, but help my unbelief!" If not, you need to be writing a book entitled *Perfect Faith and How I Attained It.*

Jesus once told His disciples that if they had the faith of a grain of mustard seed, they could move mountains (Matthew 17:20). That is an extremely encouraging statement. This verse prompts us to pray. It gives us hope when facing the impossible. But it is also a testament to the pathetic degree of faith held by most of God's people. That Jesus makes the measure so miniscule for Him to work through our lives shows that He knows our frame and realizes that we could not do much better. In Luke 18:8, Jesus asks, when He comes again, will He find faith on the earth? Wow! Is it that bad? Is it getting worse? Hasn't it always been true that vibrant faith is a rare commodity? If any of us progress to any degree of vibrant faith, it is due to the grace of God in our lives. It is because we beg Him to break through our human frailty to fortify us with that which we do not have. Most commonly, we are desperately lacking in faith. Especially in affliction, we are so susceptible to doubting.

Asaph was writing about a common "Christian" experience. His words prove that those dedicated to full-time service for God are not immune to it. In fact, they may be more susceptible to secret doubts than others since they are held to such a high standard of evident faith. How could they ever say, "Please pray for me, I am doubting the goodness of God!"? They could say it, but would they keep their jobs for long if they repeated such a notion? Also, full-time Christian servants live with the fear of the scandalous fallout that such a thing would cause in the church. What a burden to bear. Where does one go to relieve such inner turmoil? Thank God there is a place to go!

Thank God, Psalm 73 does not stop with the problem and leave us without the solution. Thank God, Asaph knew where to go and what to do. He went into the sanctuary of God. What does that mean? What did that mean for him? What does that mean for us?

HELP FOR YOUR SECRET DOUBTS

Questions

Read Psalm 142 and refer to the noted verses for these questions.

1. Do you think David was dealing with secret doubts? Clue: When David was in the cave, were there others with Him (cf. 1 Samuel 22:1–2 and 24:1–7)? Why, then, could he not express his doubts openly?

2. Since there was no one in which he could confide, where did he go to express his perplexing thoughts?

3. How did he describe his inner turmoil (verse 7)?

4. Have you ever felt that way? When and why?

5. What statements in the psalm indicate that David anticipated relief and victory over his thoughts?

Thought

God does not desire to hear presumptuous accusations against Him. It was for doing such a thing that God consigned the nation of Israel to wander in the wilderness for forty years—and many died there. Yet God *does* want to hear our perplexing thoughts and troubles. We may not be able to express them to those around us, but He is listening.

CHAPTER EIGHT

THE SANCTUARY REVELATION

Until I went into the sanctuary of God; then understood I their end.—PSALM 73:17

Verse 17 is a transition if ever there was one—a climactic statement that leaps off the page. For sixteen long verses, Asaph had declared his doubts. For sixteen long verses, he had aired out his emotional laundry. And then, a turning point—Asaph records that he went into the sanctuary and found a new perspective. If only all of us would find that same perspective. If only all of us could go into that same sanctuary. There his doubts began to disappear. There his confidence in God was restored. Where is this sanctuary? Where do we have to go to find what Asaph found?

The good news is that Asaph could not have been talking exclusively about the Temple in Jerusalem. If he were, the application would fall short. None of us would be able to go there since that sanctuary has long since been destroyed. There is no way that Asaph meant that all he had to do was go to a particular place. In fact, we know that Asaph worked in Temple service. He probably worked there on a regular, if not daily, basis. Nehemiah 12:46 makes a reference to Asaph as "chief of the singers." The previous verse records that "the singers and porters kept the ward of their God" or, in other words, kept the watch in the Temple. The Temple was the unique location of the special presence of God in Israel.

There is a possibility that it was at the Temple where Asaph received the wisdom that he needed. But, Asaph most assuredly was not saying that he discovered this revelation simply by being there. It is more reasonable to think that when he said he went into the sanctuary of God, he was speaking in an emblematic way of entering into the presence of God through meditation on God's Word and through prayer. The truth of God impacted his heart during a time of worship and communion. He was spiritually taken to the realm of God in order to receive this personal revelation. This was the sanctuary to which he referred.

That Asaph presents this experience as such an epiphany portrays a wonderful, positive truth. The positive truth is that God can enlighten our spiritual senses to the personal presence of Him in our lives and prepare our hearts to receive the wisdom of His Word. In our day, this does not have to be an audible experience, as if we physically hear God's voice. I don't think it was for Asaph either; although the Old Testament records frequent references to God speaking in this way. In the New Testament era, we have the completed Bible, which is able to make us "thoroughly furnished unto all good works" (2 Timothy 3:17). We also have the Holy Spirit dwelling in our hearts, who is there to guide us and teach us by applying God's Word to our hearts. It is an inward spiritual impression of wisdom that we need, not a direct audible expression from God. True believers are "*led* by the Spirit of God" (Romans 8:14).

First John 2:27 makes a definitive statement on this point. John says to fellow believers, "But the anointing which ye have received of him abideth in you, and ye need not that any man teach you: but as the same anointing teacheth you of all things, and is truth, and is no lie, and even as it hath taught you, ye shall abide in him." There is so much here, but I will limit my commentary to a couple of thoughts.

First, this verse says that we do not have to pray for an anointing in our era because it abides *in* us. Anointing in the Bible is emblematic of the endowment of the Holy Spirit. In this case, the anointing is the teaching ministry of the indwelling Holy Spirit in our hearts. How else could it dwell in us? The Holy Spirit dwells within us (Romans 8:9; 1 Corinthians 6:19, 12:13; 2 Corinthians 1:22; etc.). This indwelling anointing must refer to His ministry.

Also, when John says that we do not need any man to teach us, he was, in this context, referring to the fact that true believers are already convinced that Jesus is the Christ (1 John 2:19–24). He had a particular doctrine in view. He is certainly not saying that the ministry of human teachers is useless. Other places in Scripture demonstrate that we can benefit from other human teachers who have the same anointing. What he may be saying is that any time we are taught by a teacher of the Word of God, their ministry is secondary since it is the Holy Spirit who is applying the truth of God to our hearts. He is doing the teaching, albeit by using a human instrument to expound the Word. It is the Holy Spirit then who will help us to discern the truth in that which we are being taught. He is the one who convinced us that Jesus is the Christ, and His indwelling presence ensures our perseverance in that same conviction. He is the one who teaches us to abide in Christ. He is the one who imparts wisdom to us from the mind of Christ. The Holy Spirit speaks to us through the Word of God and makes God's Word known to us. He is the one who makes God's presence real to us. Since we have the Holy Spirit in our hearts and the Word of God in our hands, we can enter into the sanctuary now, today, anytime we wish. If we do, God will bring to bear His revelation upon our hearts and minds to make our doubts disappear.

The negative truth from this passage is that, like Asaph, you and I can operate around the tangible trappings of the service of God for a time and still be missing something. We can miss deep, meaningful fellowship with God. We can be there in body without really entering by way of the Spirit. Our bodies are called the temple of God today

(1 Corinthians 6:19). The local church is called the house of God today (1 Timothy 3:15). So, not only do we carry God's special presence with us, but we enter another unique manifestation of God's special presence in the church. In fact, Jesus said, where two or three are gathered in His name, He is in the midst of them (Matthew 18:20). We do not even have to go to a big church with all the bells and whistles to experience this. Yet, so many Christians enter into long seasons of doubt. Why? The problem is that we can be in the physical sanctuary (so to speak) without entering into the spiritual sanctuary. We can participate in a religious service without the presence of God and His Word powerfully stirring our souls to convince us, convict us, and change us by the truth. This inner sanctum interaction with God only happens by desperate dependence upon God—through passionate prayer from a humble and seeking heart. We have to draw nigh to God and He will draw nigh to us. We have to cleanse our hands, purify our hearts, and tune out the world to tune into God's Word (James 4:8).

This sanctuary revelation can become remote and infrequent if we are not careful. Our tendency is to become so accustomed to the rituals and religious motions of the Christian life that we lose our awareness of God Himself, and we lose the deep desire for Him and His truth.

This is especially challenging for those who work in the ministry full-time. Those in full-time ministry run the danger of justifying their lack of vitality in devotional time with God simply because of their official relationship to God's work. Like Asaph, the deeper we move into the forest of bare religion, the harder it is to see God through the trees. We think that religion is supposed to accentuate the view, and yet at times, it seems to do nothing but get in the way.

James indicates that real religion is to be an outgrowth of worship to God. It is a *result*, not a *cause*. It is the effect of looking into the "perfect law of liberty"—seeing yourself for who you are and God for who He is. It is that spiritual transaction that works its way out in the way we speak, the way we serve others, and the way we live in the world (James 1:22–27).

I had to learn this the hard way. As I said in the opening, I was reared in a pastor's home. This provided great privilege for me, but it also presented unique challenges. For most of my growing-up years, our family lived next door to the church building. We lived in a parsonage that was just a short walk away. The parking lot was our playground. The auditorium was a play place as well. My brother, sister, and I would take turns at hide and seek among the pews. I hate to admit it, but on a few occasions, we even used the baptistery as our swimming pool. It felt as if we lived at church. It was hard to distinguish when regular life ended and church life began. Our teen group met in the basement of our house. We had family meals and functions in the basement of the church. Church was home. Home was church. I also went to a Christian school, so most of my time was spent in a completely Christian culture. I had Christian teachers. I hung around Christian friends. I could walk the walk and talk "Christianese" at will. I ate Christian cereal for breakfast and Christian hot dogs for lunch. (Okay…maybe not, but you know what I mean.) That is not all bad, but because of this, I learned the part of outward public conformity with little inward and private communion with God.

Late in high school, the sham started to show. I got into some trouble that revealed the true condition of my heart. This was a turning point for me. I could not put on a show anymore. If I was going to be known once again as a genuine Christian, it would take steps of personal sanctification to restore an image that had been lost. This time it had to be real. I searched my heart. I was truly a born-again believer. I knew that, at age nine, I had truly repented of my sinful condition before God and had trusted only in Jesus and His work for my salvation. The desire to please Jesus was always there in my heart. I had acted upon that desire from time to time. I had just not learned that there was so much more to the Christian life than that which surrounds it.

God worked in my heart to attend a Christian college after high school; and it was there that I learned to get alone with God, to commune with Him in order to fuel my faith, guide my thoughts, and direct my steps. I had a fresh start. No one knew me as a pastor's kid. I was in a new environment. I was facing monumental decisions. I was heading toward adult life. It was during that crucial period that I realized my desperate need for God. Through it all, I learned how to get into the sanctuary. I learned to walk with God in His Word and through prayer.

Now, in the ministry, I have dedicated myself to spending quality time with God. I make it a daily endeavor. I heard a pastor say once, "I am resolved never to let my professional success ever get ahead of my personal sanctification." I'll never forget those words. One thing that having cancer has done for me is to increase my awareness of this commitment on a more consistent basis. I have to stay close to God all the time. In the midst of adversity, I am more susceptible to doubts. Like Asaph, I have learned that when doubts come, there is only one place to go—into the sanctuary of God; and I can enter that place on my knees, at my desk, at church, or anywhere I am willing to seek a real connection with God. So can you.

HELP FOR YOUR SECRET DOUBTS

Questions

1. What should we long to see in our sanctuary experience (Psalm 63:2)?

2. Is this experience limited to the physical house of God? Has it ever been (Psalm 63:5–8)?

3. Where do we learn God's way (Psalm 77:13)? Think of a time when you have swerved off the path of God's perfect will. What was one of the reasons this happened?

4. How should you respond to the revelation of the presence of God in your life (Psalm 134:2)?

5. What does it take to draw close to God so that this can occur (James 4:6–10)?

Thought

We can have a sanctuary experience today. In the New Testament, we are invited by God to draw close to Him through the ministry of the Holy Spirit in prayer and in the Word. When we are close to God, truths come into view—truths that were not as clear before. These glimpses of God and His wisdom are what we need to go forward by faith.

CHAPTER NINE

THE RETRIBUTION OF THE WICKED

Surely thou didst set them in slippery places: thou castedst them down into destruction. How are they brought down into desolation, as in a moment! They are utterly consumed with terrors. As a dream when one awaketh; so, O Lord, when thou awaketh, thou shalt despise their image.—PSALM 73:18–20

At the end of verse 17, Asaph said that his sanctuary revelation gave him a new perspective concerning the wicked. He was able to understand their "end." Through the eyes of faith, he was able to see the ultimate justice of God on those who willfully disobey Him and disregard His grace in their lives. In verses 18 and 19, he said that he saw the wicked in "slippery places" about to experience God's judgment "as in a moment." In verse 20, Asaph goes on to say that when God awakes or decides in time to punish the wicked, it happens suddenly and results in their utter destruction, being "consumed with terrors." This is strong language. You could say that Asaph received a vision of Hell.

This descriptive revelation mirrors that which is found in Psalm 37. There David tells believers in God not to envy the wicked, because someday soon the wicked will be "cut down" by God (verses 1–2). He refers us to the perspective of God, who sees the future day of judgment for the wicked (verse 13). God also sees the ultimate blessing of the righteous, whose "inheritance shall be forever" (verse 18). This was the perspective that God gave Asaph in the sanctuary. He was given the faith-filled foresight to see the ultimate retribution of God for the wicked and the ultimate blessing of God for the righteous.

With this understanding, how could he then continue to envy the evildoers around him? This perception changed everything about how he looked at them. He saw them now as objects of pity, not desire. Being aware of God's sure and ultimate justice became a new lens through which Asaph was able to look at the unbelieving world.

The doctrine of God's ultimate justice is detestable to some. They are baffled by the existence of evil in the first place. "Why would a supposedly good God allow evil to exist in His universe?" they ask. Beyond that, they bristle at the idea that God is going to banish men and women from Him forever in a place of perpetual fire. This doctrine that became such a comfort to Asaph is a source of consternation and repulsion to others.

Many books have been written about the existence of evil and the justice of God. I have studied a few of them. Let me add my two cents and share that which I have come to understand in its elementary form, so we can reach some degree of clarity together within this short context.

Before we can come to receive what the Bible says about evil, it may be good to become aware of the vacuous nature of the alternative views. Some teach that evil is ethereal. To them, it is either an impersonal force or an illusion. Lacking objective grounds to define it, they just relate it to some negative experience of human life whether real or imaginary. This concept does not correspond with what we see in reality.

The Bible does not say that evil is some rogue force lacking specificity. The Bible says that evil is personal. This corresponds to that which we witness in the world. Evil began in the heart of Satan and came into the heart of man as a prideful objection to the goodness of God and His will. Evil has passed to all through an inherent nature that contains the capability and propensity to reject the moral standards of God. Evil is specified as being the direct opposite of God's pure character. It is defined against that one true infinite and objective standard. We have all fallen short of that glorious and majestic measurement (Romans 3:10, 23). There is no way to escape it—evil finds its roots in the human heart. Evil is inside of us and has corrupted the world around us.

Some reject that notion on naturalistic grounds. They say that evil is environmental. In other words, every society can decide its own moral framework. The "wrongness" of an action is determined by what any given society views as negative to the propagation of their group and the human species in general. This is moral relativism for sure. On such subjective grounds, the naturalist has no business condemning any behavior. If we are operating on that basis, and within the framework of natural selection, then how can anything truly be called "wrong," "negative," or "immoral"? If nature is simply taking its course, who are we (as a group or as individuals) to judge what is negative or degrading? If all things are a product of time and chance, and we as humans are simply an accidental accumulation of atoms, then we should just let our chemical and biological processes lead us to whatever impulses and actions they produce, and no one should pass judgment on the outcome.

This environmental view of evil does not make sense to me. Instinctively, it does not make sense to anyone, even to those who profess to believe it. Even the naturalist does not live out his own worldview in this regard. He ascribes objective value in relation to people and their behaviors. All of us have a sense of morality. We have a moral compass called a conscience. It is informed and influenced by our environment in one direction or another, but it issues from God alone and is measured by and according to His pure character. God gave us this metaphysical mechanism, and we act either according to or in denial of it.

We are capable of evil; God is not (James 1:13). He is good and always does that which is right. Why then would He allow evil to exist in His universe? As I have stated before, one of the reasons that God created the condition for it to exist is so that man could exercise His will to choose. God presented to man two opposite poles: obedience and disobedience, privilege and restriction. Without opposing options, there would be no choice to make. If you go to a soda machine and all there is to buy is root beer, do you really have a choice if you want something to drink? Without a real choice, mankind could not fellowship with God in a willful way. God presented the options, and one led to evil. God uses the presence of evil in the universe to display a full array of attributes—like grace, mercy, justice, and sacrificial love—attributes that we may not recognize without their opposites also in motion (Romans 9:22–23).

The essence of wickedness is to disregard the option for obedience and fellowship to do the opposite. God would not be holy and just if He did not deal with this blatant offense. He did. He allowed mankind to feel the full sting of living on an earth that has been corrupted by the presence of sin. God is perfectly just. He would not have been so unless the personal punishment matched the crime as well. Sin corrupts all that comes in contact with it. Sin is eternal in its compounding effect. It affects those who have an eternal soul. Its damage is etched in time and in an eternal history. And ultimately, sin is an offense against an eternal God. Because of this, sin incurs an everlasting consequence in a place completely isolated from the goodness of God. This is a just recompense similar to our penalty of life sentence in prison without the possibility of parole. We understand on earth that crimes with unremitting life-long results deserve an unremitting life-long penalty. When we sin, we are choosing to do that which separates us from communion with God. Barring some supernatural rectitude or Divine pardon, this is an eternal charge that results in eternal separation from God.

God is gracious, and he has made a way of reconciliation. He has manifested His unique majesty and glory in creation. We all know in our hearts that there must be an infinite, personal, and intelligent first cause. To think otherwise is to deny the obvious. The universe is not infinite and personal. The universe is made up of its constituent parts. It did not create itself. There must be a transcendent Creator God that created the universe and all that dwells in it. And only the Bible contains revelation about a being that has the character and credentials to be such a one. In the Bible, God says that we can begin to discover Him if we respond to the general revelation in creation. God says that if we believe that He is and diligently seek Him, He will reward us with revelation concerning Himself (Hebrews 11:6). God obligates Himself to bring the sincere seeker to the final revelation of His words in the Bible where one can know how to be pardoned from sin's penalty through faith in the death and resurrection of Jesus Christ. The "wicked" (in the full, official sense) are those who walk away from God's drawing influence. They refuse to know Jesus and to worship Him in spirit and in truth.

God sees the end from the beginning. He knows who the "wicked" are. He does not bring them to their just punishment immediately. He allows them the superficial enjoyment of this life. He confirms a condition present in their own hearts and minds by letting them act according to their deviant desires. It can seem, for a short season, as if they are getting by. (Ultimately, this is God's longsuffering and grace, giving those who reject Him continued time to repent—2 Peter 3:9).

The current prosperity of the wicked can be a source of confusion for those who have been reconciled to God and enjoy communion with Him. Asaph is not alone in his bewilderment. We all need not only a revelation of Heaven but also a revelation of Hell. We need to be aware of both God's blessing and His judgment. When we are acutely aware of God's ultimate justice, it changes the way we look at those around us. We are not so attracted to the activities and lifestyles of the wicked. We are less likely to covet them and their ways. We are more likely to pity them. When their wickedness affects us, we are more apt to forgive. We are able to forbear. We are not stirred up to pursue personal revenge. Vengeance is God's job. We are not so wronged by the wrongs. We are not so troubled by the troubles. We see the end.

Asaph went into the sanctuary, and this is what he saw: the wicked are walking on a slippery slope. At any moment they could be vaulted into Hell. This was a transformative thought for him. Such a revelation can be an epiphany for us as well. We have to see the end to deal with the present. We have to believe that in time God will bring to light the hidden works of darkness in order to set the crooked things straight. Add to this the awareness of God's ultimate blessing upon those who have received His reconciliation (which Asaph discusses later), and we now have the spiritual resources necessary to silence our secret doubts. We now have what it takes to conquer our inclination to doubt God and His goodness. When we come to this awareness, we look back at our former doubtful thoughts with displeasure and disdain. We will say to ourselves, "What in the world was I thinking?"

HELP FOR YOUR SECRET DOUBTS

Questions

1. According to Proverbs 22:19–20, why should we not envy evil men? Why is this such a challenge?

2. How should we respond to evil men according to verses 24–25 of the same chapter?

3. According to Ephesians 5:11, what should be the extent of the Christian's association with the morally degrading aspects of our culture?

4. In what way does the grace of God motivate us to live according to Titus 2:11–14? What characteristics are associated with a life lived by the grace of God? Do you think that we will live this way if we are envying the wicked?

5. Read Psalm 9:17. With this understanding, is there anything to envy about a wicked person's life?

Thought

We must see the end of wickedness in order to look at it in disgust. We must look at the unbelieving wicked as objects of pity and not of aspiration. This is impossible unless God, in grace, motivates our lives with an eternal perspective.

CHAPTER TEN

I'M AS DUMB AS AN OX!

Thus my heart was grieved, and I was pricked in my veins. So foolish was I, and ignorant: I was as a beast before thee.— PSALM 73:21–22

Being convicted by God can be a humbling experience. When we are struck with a sense of God's presence and the majestic nature of His infinite wisdom, we realize how ignorant we really are. After Asaph's sanctuary experience, he began to understand how foolish he had been in doubting God. He described his conviction as a piercing source of grief in his heart (Psalm 73:21). Then he said in an amazing self-degrading manner, "*So foolish was I, and ignorant: I was as a beast before thee.*" In other words, "I'm as dumb as an ox!"

Animals are obviously much less intelligent than humans. They act by basic reflex and instinct. There is no deep reasoning within them. There is no introspection. An animal does not take time to meditate or ponder. We act as animals when we respond to life's situations in an impulsive, emotional way. It is at these times that we doubt God—when we have not taken the time to consider His character, His Word, and His power. We are just reacting to our problems. When we once again get a glimpse of God's sublime sovereignty, we realize how dumb it is to question God's infinite wisdom. When God's Word shines in our hearts, once again, our rash thoughts seem so childish and immature. We say to ourselves, "What was I thinking? My dog is smarter than to question God."

Job experienced such a debasing moment. In his pain, he began to question God and His goodness. In the thirty-first chapter of the book of the Bible named after him, Job lists his moral accomplishments. He does not directly say it, but it is as if he is saying to God, "Look at how good I have lived! Why has so much trouble come my way? I don't deserve all of this!" Then he calls out to God to answer him. What gall! What presumption! He talks as if God owes him an explanation. God does not owe any of us an explanation. Even if He did try to explain to us the intricate purposes of His eternal plan, we could not understand it. It would be like trying to explain advanced calculus to a two year old. We are finite. God's wisdom is infinite. God in grace did respond to Job—not with answers but with questions. He starts with, "Where were you when I made the world? Tell me how I did it." (Job 38:4–6, my paraphrase). God then asks Job to explain one creative act after another. Job 40:4 records that Job responds by saying, "Behold, I am vile; what shall I answer thee? I will lay my hand upon my mouth." I love it. Job essentially said to God, "I've got nothing intelligent to say. I think I'll just shut up." God kept on speaking to Job, asking him to account for His acts of creation if he were able. When God decided that He had said enough, Job finally acknowledged with a sense of abject lowliness, "…I uttered…things too wonderful for me, which I knew not…Wherefore I abhor myself, and repent in dust and ashes" (Job 42:3, 6).

As mere mortals prone to delusion, we think we are so smart sometimes. We think we know how things should go. We think we can explain the inexplicable. We think we have mental wherewithal to cast doubt upon God. There are even people who think that they are smart enough to doubt the presence of God altogether. They call themselves "atheist" or "agnostic." Some of the most apt doubters and deniers have Ph.D.s beside their names. We must admire their educational effort. But have they become "too smart for their own britches" (as my mother would say)? God's wisdom is from everlasting to everlasting; and yet, these supposedly high scholars believe that they have accumulated enough human knowledge in their short existence to declare God unnecessary and unreal. Every time they open their mouths to explain the existence of the universe, they reveal how small-minded they really are. They couch their imprudence in the midst of lofty terms such as "cosmic inflation" and "quantum fluctuation." Although there may be some truth in these cosmological constructs, the theoretical premises and conclusions made by most who promote them are unwarranted and unwise. They essentially are telling us that the universe blew into existence from infinite nothingness. If there were a "Big Bang," it was the sound of God's resounding voice as He created the universe from nothing (Genesis 1:3; Hebrews 11:3). The universe is telling us that it had a beginning in time, but those who doubt God can't see beyond that to God. In truth, they don't want to see or believe the obvious—there must be an infinite and personal first cause (2 Peter 3:5). Many God deniers say that inanimate objects spontaneously produced all the living things we see around us. We are amazed by their mental dexterity in trying to explain the nonsensical. We respect their intent to greater learning, but as it relates to true wisdom, they are missing something essential. They are missing the necessity for divinity. They are missing God. There's no respect in that. I realize that this sounds harsh, but God said it even more distinctly when He declared in His Word, "The fool hath said in his heart, There is no God." In fact, in order that no one could confuse His thoughts on this, He said it twice (Psalm 14:1; 53:1). God has made His stance clear. Doubting Him is fool's ground.

As Christians, we would never entertain such nonsense—or would we? What's worse—to question God's existence or to question whether or not He knows what He is doing? Both stem from a state of delusion. Both are personal affronts against an all-powerful God. It's not smart to do either. So why do we do it?

We doubt God when we focus on our problems. Our range of normal vision is so limited to the small context in which we live. It is hard with natural eyes to see anything other than what affects our little lives. We are so bound to this earth. Transcendent thoughts are unnatural. The big picture is so obscure. Most of the time, our thoughts are confined to the situation at hand. Our hurts are all-consuming. Pain is so tangible. Like a magnet, the problems we face are a strong force to attract the sole focus of our judgment. Our perceptions are skewed by our situations. When things go well, we think well of God; when things go bad, our thoughts of God suddenly shift in the opposite direction.

If we are not diligent and careful, we will find that this tendency affects our whole conception of God. We are not here for God, we surmise; He is there for us. We assume that doing right will always produce positive results as we define them. We presume that God's justice on evildoers should always be immediate, especially when they have done evil to us or in a way that affects us. We think that God should move in ways that are pleasant to us—in ways that do not deny our selfish sense of comfort. In short, when things go south, we become disappointed in God. In turn, we think that we know better than God on how things ought to be.

In a clear-minded moment, it is easier to see how foolish this is. God can give us that clarity. In the sanctuary, clarity can and will happen. It requires a strong, convicting influence of God and His Word to erase the doubts from our minds, but there, in a place close to God, the removal takes place. When the wisdom from God does come to us, it sheds the light on those dull thoughts that once consumed our minds. We feel so sorry for ever thinking them.

Doubting God can become a habit if we let it. Over and over, as we respond in the same questioning manner, a pattern sets into our psyche. The most dangerous condition establishes itself when we no longer are aware that we are thinking this way. Our default position is always negative. We go there so quickly that it is almost imperceptible. We may still believe in God, but in practice we have become atheists. A negative response to life's circumstances reveals a lack of trust in God.

As a pastor, I have dealt with people who don't even seem to realize that almost every word out of their mouth is conditioned negativity. I hesitate to ask these people how they are doing with anything specific or how they are doing in general. What I get is some variety of sour pickles. I want to say, "Do you really believe in God? Then why do you act and talk as if He does not exist?" If we really trust God, we will have a positive outlook. If we really trust God, we will act in a productive manner by seeking His face for solutions, strength, and deliverance. Otherwise, we might just as well join the ranks of the life-long skeptics.

Momentary and occasional doubting is understandable for the child of God. We are weak. We are frail. None of us operate with perfect faith. But a Christian who consistently doubts God is acting worse than an animal. At least an animal is oblivious. We should know better.

Doubting is a serious issue. As believers, we need to ask God to remove any vestige of this disease from our spiritual lives. In Psalm 73, Asaph confessed doubting for what it really is—foolishness and ignorance. Once his heart was cleansed and his doubting spirit was removed, a new glowing disposition took its place.

HELP FOR YOUR SECRET DOUBTS

Questions

1. What do the "heavens" tell us according to Psalm 19:1?

2. Is this message universal (cf. with Romans 1:20)?

3. If a person does not recognize God, and will not come to the place of having a personal relationship with Him, what is the main reason (Psalm 10:4)?

4. What else do the heavens declare to us (Psalm 97:6)? In other words, the same God who has the power and wisdom to create and sustain the universe certainly knows how things should rightly operate in this life.

5. When you doubt that God knows what He is doing, where should you look for some perspective?

Thought

Go out on a starry night sometime. Set your gaze on the heavens. How in the world can we question a God who is able to put what we see into motion and hold it all in place? It does not take much to realize how foolish it is to doubt God. This exercise alone can do it. For that reason, we should make it a continual practice. Read and reflect on Psalm 8; as you do this, it will increase your awe of God and lead you into His presence.

CHAPTER ELEVEN

THE REWARD OF THE RIGHTEOUS

> *Nevertheless I am continually with thee: thou hast holden me by my right hand. Thou shalt guide me with thy counsel, and afterward receive me to glory. Whom have I in heaven but thee? And there is none upon earth that I desire beside thee. My flesh and my heart faileth; but God is the strength of my heart, and my portion for ever.*—Psalm 73:23–26

Due to Asaph's sanctuary experience, he was able to give an amazing testimony in verses 23–26. Asaph basically testified to the fact that God had become his everything. This is the believer's goal in this life—to come to the place where we find our fulfillment for this life in God alone and look forward to being with Him more than anything else. In verse 23, Asaph says that since his episode of doubting was over, he could sense God's constant presence and care. He said that God was holding him with His right hand. As Christians today, can we actually get to the place where we sense God's support around us? I submit that, like Asaph, we can. This is not to say that we feel something or have a mystical experience. When we know God is with us, there is within us a spiritual sense of emotional undergirding. God is holding us up. He is lifting our spirits above the standard state of conditional responses. We are giving praise when we should be going nuts. We are letting go when usually we would be tightening our grip. We are full of faith when the circumstances in our lives seem to be working in a way contrary to the goodness of God. The initial reward of the righteous is at first the blessing of the strengthening support of God.

What is ironic about this awareness is that it is heightened by a state of physical weakness. It is enhanced by trouble. To a greater degree, we spiritually sense God's hand of support when forms of physical support prove insufficient. In 2 Corinthians 12:7–8, we read where the Apostle Paul prayed to God three times to remove a painful physical infirmity. In verse 9, we read God's response to Paul: "My grace is sufficient for thee; for my strength is made perfect in weakness." What follows is one of the most astounding testimonies in the Scriptures. Paul said, "Most gladly therefore will I rather glory in my infirmities, that the power of Christ may rest upon me." And if that were not enough, he adds, "Therefore

I take pleasure in infirmities, in reproaches, in necessities, in persecutions, in distresses for Christ's sake: for when I am weak, then am I strong" (verses 9–10). Whoa! How could he say that? Was Paul a closet sadist? Was he a glutton for pain? No, he was upheld by the right hand of God. Paul came to realize the reward of living life in close communion with God and resting secure in Him alone. You can't buy that blessing with all the money in the world.

When we accept this truth, nothing else in this world can hold such inspiring attraction. In Psalm 73:24, Asaph said that in this life God would guide him with counsel and afterward receive him to glory. Before the sanctuary revelation, Asaph was looking around for parity and satisfaction. He wanted what others had. He wanted more. He wanted his just due. After the sanctuary experience, he began once again to look to God for guidance and ahead to glory in Heaven. He looked for guidance now, glory later. What a way to live!

In view of the spectrum of eternity, life on earth is a miniscule dot. Compared to the eternal state after death, life here is so short that it is almost without recognition. Our lives on earth are like a "tale that is told" (Psalm 90:9). Our lives are like a momentary vapor—a puff of smoke (James 4:14). All we need in this short life is enough guidance, support, and strength to know that God is there for us. All we need from God is enough to get us through. We are bound to God Himself. We are bound for glory. What else do we need? If it takes temporal weakness and deprivation to liberate us from ourselves so that we can yearn for God and all that He has prepared for us in

Heaven, so be it. If we could only lose our lives for Christ's sake, we could truly find them (Matthew 10:39).

Asaph was able to see God alone as his complete source of satisfaction in this life and in the life to come. He said in verse 25 that there was no one in Heaven or earth that he desired besides God. This is not to say that he had no other loving human relations. Asaph was also not implying that he held no natural care for anyone in this life or who had gone to the next. This was simply a statement of priority. Once Asaph became deeply aware of the presence of God and His leading in his life, he was able to see that no human relationship could provide what only God could provide. The source of so much dissatisfaction comes to us when, we, like Asaph, for a time seek satisfaction in those things that cannot fully satisfy. We expect wealth and possessions to satisfy. We expect effort to pay off for us with lasting soulful appreciation. We look to people to provide wholeness for us. What we find is that there is no fulfillment in any earthly thing or in any human relationship.

We were made in the image of God. That image is diminished by the curse of sin, and only God can restore what was lost. God is self-sufficient. He does not need "stuff" to prop up His personal well-being. God has an eternal relational nature consistent in the Trinity. He is a complex unity. He is one, and yet made up of three distinct persons—Father, Son, and Holy Spirit. As such, and being perfect, He is completely satisfied and sustained in Himself and with Himself. Being made in God's likeness, we have a relational nature. We not only have a relational nature, but we also have a relational need. Ultimately, we were made to fellowship with God and enjoy the ministry of each member of the Trinity. In God, we have a father, a brother, a comforter; we have a protector, a friend, and a counselor. In Him, we have all that we need for wholeness and so much more. Heaven will be Heaven because He is there, and we will not be distracted by any lesser longings besides those that lead to Him alone. Whatever happened in the "sanctuary," one thing is certain: Asaph was able to see God alone as His true reward.

In summarizing this thought, Asaph stated that although his flesh and his heart were failing, God was the strength of his heart and his portion forever (verse 26). In the midst of human frailty—a frailty that leads to doubt and envy—Asaph was able to see God strengthen his spirit. Not only that, but Asaph was able to see God as his all in all. This is a rarefied ground for believers. Not many get to this place. Sometimes, it takes extreme affliction to arrive at this state of celestial comprehension. It takes a trial strong enough to cause a person to see the weak and temporal nature of all earthly attachments.

Without meaning to sound particularly pious, I think I am getting there. I am sensing a change in my spirit. The things that were so important to me in the past do not seem as vital as they used to seem. I am learning that God must be my portion. I am realizing this truth as my portion in this life seems to be running through my fingertips.

Cancer has been an excellent teacher for me. I used to value my health. I exercised. I was active. I loved to run. My running days are over. Due to the cancer, my spine has been damaged beyond repair. I cannot lift anything over twenty pounds. Even when I am not bending over, my back will "lock up" without warning. This is extremely humbling. Recently at the airport, my petite little wife had to carry all our family's luggage to the ticket counter. People were looking at me. I could read their thoughts: "Why is that guy making that poor girl carry everything?!" When I go to the store and buy a larger item, I have to ask someone to carry it for me. This is humbling as well. I used to value my looks. I prided myself in having hair that was almost never out of place. My cancer treatments took my hair from me for a time. I was taking a shower one day when all of a sudden clumps of hair began to fall down to the drain. You could say that my vanity was being washed down the drain as well. I was humiliated. I could not relate to the person I saw in the mirror. When I went back to church for the first time after my stem cell transplant, the people I loved were supportive. They told me how good I looked. I could tell that they were just trying to make me feel better. A few months later, when little sprigs of hair began to grow again, one lady came out with her true feelings. She said, "You know, Pastor, sometimes it has to get worse before it gets better." My hair has grown back since then, but it is not the same. I am balding naturally as well.

Hair is so superficial, isn't it? But it represents something deeper and we all know it. What was happening was that my sense of security was being shaken. I always thought that I would live a long life into old age. I now know that it's all relative. I may still live to be eighty. At this point, that seems to be a distant dream not worth dreaming. I do want to see my children grow up. I would love to walk McKayla down the aisle. But I cannot presume upon the future. I have to live today. I have learned through cancer that life on earth is not trustworthy. I am living on borrowed time. I must look to eternity to find my portion. I must look to that which only an eternal God can provide.

My wife has been with me through all of the trials. She is a gift from God. I want to be clear here. When God becomes your portion, this does not mean that you cannot value other things. In fact, it is God who gives us every good gift and all good things to richly enjoy (James 1:17, 1 Timothy 6:17). Besides my salvation, Stacie is God's greatest blessing to me. I can be myself with her. She loves me. She accepts me. She puts up with me. Stacie is a steady influence in my life. She is my partner in family, in work, and in ministry. My greatest moments of fun and pleasure have been with her. There have been some frustrating moments as well. Over time, I have come to realize the temporal nature of our relationship. I have been on the edge and have seen the limits. I can in no way presume upon her for absolute affection or impose on her my greatest needs. Only God can satisfy my soul. Only God can share with me the timeless treasure of contentment. And contentment only comes when God is enough.

That's what Asaph meant when he said that there was no one on earth and no one in Heaven that he desired but God. I can imagine that this sounds so "spiritual" to some—so otherworldly and idealistic. For a person who does not even have a relationship with God, what Asaph describes is so far from their experience. To the skeptic who thinks this perspective impossible, I would suggest that not only is it possible, but it is essential. We were created to bring pleasure to God and commune with Him forever. No other reason for living carries with it essential purpose. We were made for God. God is the beginning and end of all we are. Asaph's journey from doubt to this discovery is recorded so we can know that God's sufficiency is ours to claim. God is our compensation for life itself. He is our "portion." And we know that God, in grace, has squelched our secret doubts when we come to realize that amazing truth.

HELP FOR YOUR SECRET DOUBTS

Questions

1. How great is the sum of God's thoughts towards us according to Psalm 139:17–18? Can that same thing be said to describe any human relationship? Does anyone love us more than God?

2. What will be the extent of God's restoration project to prepare for the eternal state (Revelation 21:1)?

3. The New Jerusalem is the centerpiece of this new creation. What is the most attractive aspect of this new dwelling place (Revelation 21:2–3; 22–24)?

4. What will Jesus bring with Him when He comes again (Revelation 22:12)?

5. Do you think that anyone or anything on earth can compete with that which is waiting for us in God's eternal realm?

Thought

God Himself is our greatest reward. He loves us like no one else does. He is preparing a place for us that is so glorious it will require a new earth and a new universe to be its majestic backdrop and to frame its beauty. If we, as believers, could only get a small glimpse of this, we would never envy the wicked.

CHAPTER TWELVE

IT'S ALL GOOD!

For, lo, they that are far from thee shall perish: thou hast destroyed all them that go a whoring from thee. But it is good for me to draw near to God: I have put my trust in the Lord God, that I may declare all thy works.—PSALM 73:27–28

Asaph wrote the end of this psalm with confidence—no wavering here. He ends by saying, "It's all good!" Well, that's not exactly what he said, but that is what he meant. Among other things, this is a psalm of acceptance and affirmation. Whatever he was dealing with, he not only accepted it, but he now saw it as a source of goodness from God. You may be saying in your adversity and affliction, "What good is there in this?"

Since you have made it this far in your reading, I want to share with you the most sublime, liberating thought of this whole book. Here it is. Are you ready? Anything is good if it carries the potential to draw you closer to God. And since everything in life carries that potential, it's all good! Let's work this out together before we close the thoughts in this small book.

First, we see in verse 27 that Asaph repeats his conclusion about God's ultimate judgment. To him, a man who struggled with envy, this was worth repeating. This time, not only does he say that the wicked shall perish, but he says that God will judge them because of their spiritual whoredom. Asaph uses strong language to state a hard truth. Anyone who turns from seeking fulfillment in God alone is a spiritual whore. The first of the Ten Commandments says, "Thou shalt have no other gods before me" (Exodus 20:3). This is a moral law that many of us break with impunity. We worship gods of our own choosing—gods made in our image, gods that we can manipulate, gods that are manageable. We put ourselves above God. We worship ourselves. We put other people above God. We think that we need someone more than we need God. We even make gods out of things formed from materials that God made. A car, a house, a boat, and a multitude of other temporal trinkets could take the place of God as our primary desires. We are seeking satisfaction in all the wrong places. For many, their lives have devolved to the degree that they adore the least things in life—things given to them by God, and yet, things that distract them from the worship He deserves. The unbelieving wicked never turn to God from this low lifestyle. They seek any life partner but God—whether fictional, personal, or material. Ultimately, God gives them what they wanted all along—existence apart from Him and His infinite love.

God has always existed. He was made by no one and for no one. He is self-existent and self-sufficient. He does not exist for our benefit; we exist for His. We were made by God, and for His pleasure (Revelation 4:11). That's it. It's so simple, but many stumble at this transformative thought. Any true lasting benefit in life comes to us in drawing closer to Him.

Romans 11:36 is one of the most profound verses in the Bible. It makes a definitive statement on this point. Speaking of God it says, "For of him, and through him, and to him, are all things: to whom be glory forever. Amen." Who can plumb the depths of this verse? On the surface, we can at least come to know that since God is the source of all things and the creating and sustaining agent of all things, by nature, He Himself is the end of all that exists in the universe. He is both the means and the end. He is the final cause, the reason, the goal, and the fulfilling purpose of all there is. Our being is due to His. We are because He is. All human history is moving to one concluding purpose—to bring Him glory through the manifold witness of His majestic wisdom. There is an irrepressible, objective flow to the universe, and it is moving on course towards God. Those that try to swim upstream are eventually swallowed by the current. Those who willfully go with the flow find that when they do, their lives take on true meaning and purpose. They ride the waves and enjoy the ride with all of its ups and downs.

I am learning to ride the waves to God. In the last few years God has given me a renewed perspective of life. And with that, He has presented to me wonderful opportunities to declare His works. Two years ago, I endured a stem cell transplant treatment. I came through in a miraculous way. About a month after the last day of my treatment, I had the worst day, followed by a day I will never forget. I woke up in the morning feeling completely normal—no nausea, no aches, and no burdensome fatigue. I felt like a new man. I gave all the praise to God. He had given me a reprieve. People all over the country were following me on the blog that my wife had started. Countless people were sharing in my blessedness. My doctors were thrilled with my recovery. They warned me to be cautious, but I just could not contain myself. Although my immune system had been weakened, I just could not stay away from church. I jumped back into ministry. My preaching took on new fervor. I put my whole heart into each new day of service. On the fun side, I began to hit the road on my bike again. The year after my stem cell treatment, I enjoyed the wonderful experience of riding in a 25-mile charity event to raise money for cancer research. I raised $1200 through the generous gifts of many friends and family members. When I rode that day, I felt as if I could go forever.

As I write this book, I am enjoying one of the most exciting and fruitful times of my ministry. I was given the opportunity to be a guest teacher for a one credit-hour course at Yale Law School. I directed a reading course on the subject of "Judeo-Christian Principles of Early American Law." Thirteen students participated, and I was able to work with some amazing Christian students. Some of the others were searching for answers about God and searching for Christ. To share with them the truth of God's Word was an honor beyond words to express it. During this same period, we started a Bible institute at our church. Five students signed up for the inaugural semester. Our church also hosted a six-week evangelistic "Dinner and DVD" series. We had thirty guests participate, some who had never seriously studied the claims of the Bible at any time in their lives. Right now, we are in the process of purchasing a new church building. This seemed like an impossible dream when we first planted the church—now it is happening.

On the family front, since the stem cell transplant, I was able to coach my two youngest children as they played soccer. I was thrilled beyond measure to see my daughter fight through some joint pain to play on that field with all her heart. She was the best defender on the team. I was able to watch my son score again and again and witness first hand his contagious desire to win. My second oldest son has developed more in the last two years than at any time since we adopted him. Michael has a mild form of autism. We had reached a plateau in our work with him until God led us to a therapeutic program that took him to a whole new level of ability. It is remarkable how far he has come. Recently, I watched him take a green belt test in Karate. I marveled at his new dexterity and skill.

Michael still has a long way to go, and God is helping us as we help him. My oldest son is not at home. Even though he has been challenging, God is protecting him and miraculously taking care of his needs. My wife continues to serve with me in ministry and faithfully cares for our family. She enjoys sharing with others the lessons that she has learned along our journey. The trials that we share have been used by God to give her a platform for greater ministry. We still have our blessings and burdens, but we have experienced God's grace in amazing ways since my stem cell transplant.

God has used my challenges to draw me closer to Him. He is using me to a greater degree to declare His wonderful works. It is too early to say that the "Zac Curse" is lifted. We are not walking through a rose garden. Each day we face serious challenges at home and at church. One thing is for sure, God is making us acutely aware that He is working all things for His glory and our good. My life could drastically change tomorrow. My cancer could return at any time. I believe that I will be able to say, "It's all good!" I have seen how the most trying of times can become the greatest impetus to drive a person to God.

Psalm 73, a psalm of Asaph, will always speak to me. Its truths are permanently cemented in my mind and heart. In moments of doubt, its wisdom will prove victorious. I know that by God's enabling grace, I will be able to work through any wayward thoughts that may come. God helped Asaph. He will help me. God has done it before. He will do it again. As with my brother Asaph, He will draw me to Himself.

Through his circumstances, Asaph of old was moving closer to God. In Psalm 73, what started as a desperate expression of doubt became a distinct declaration of the goodness of God. In the end, Asaph got it right. It was God who helped him work through it in his mind and heart; and by inspired compulsion, he put his thoughts down in words. In so doing, he joined the collective consent of many other inspired witnesses of God. In his final verse he says from the heart, "I have put my trust in the Lord God, that I may declare all thy works." From these words we can only believe that Asaph continued his life with renewed purpose.

What is that purpose? What is it that Asaph had rediscovered? According to the last verse of the psalm, that purpose is to know God and make Him known. That is the essence of ministry. That is the essence of life.

HELP FOR YOUR SECRET DOUBTS

A Prayer

Righteous, Heavenly Father, I ask you to cleanse my heart from any distracting and degrading thoughts. Forgive me for my doubts, my envious looks, and my sinful attempts to seek full satisfaction in things apart from You. I do love You. I do believe in You and Your goodness. Help my unbelief. Shore up my spirit in the sanctuary of close communion with You and You alone. Grant to me the grace to see the end of wickedness and the blessedness of our relationship together.

Lord, You are my portion forever. I accept all that You are doing and will do to help me to see that. In moments of spiritual conflict, I ask You to do what it takes to break through the fog and give me light.

You did it for Asaph. I ask You to do it for me. In the precious name of Jesus my Savior I pray, Amen!

ACKNOWLEDGMENTS

My wife, Stacie, not only encouraged me to write this book, but also spent many hours reviewing and editing it. This book bears many marks of her expertise. I also thank my brother, Dan Zacharias; my associate pastor, Matt Fitch; my father-in-law, Michael Ashmore, Lieutenant Colonel, USAF (retired); and my good friends in the ministry: Pastor John Ludka, Pastor Sammy Frye, and Dr. Rand Hummel for advising me concerning the content found in these pages. Their help was invaluable to me in making this work as precise as possible. Finally, I thank Monica Bass and the staff of Striving Together Publications for taking this work and making it ready for the printed page. I appreciate their labor of love in giving this book its final form so that God can use it to bless His people around the globe.

ABOUT THE AUTHOR

DR. TIM ZACHARIAS is a husband and father of four children. He is the founding pastor of the Community Baptist Church of Branford, Connecticut. Tim is also a trained counselor, conference speaker, and lecturer. He has taught in many settings including the Yale Law School where he directed a course on the Christian principles of early American law.

Also available from

Striving Together Publications

The Plan B Prayer

What do you do when you've lost the ideal—when you know "Plan A" is no longer a possibility? Moses knew what it was to lose "Plan A." His response was an inspired prayer recorded as Psalm 90. It's the "Plan B" prayer, and it leads us to restored hope and purpose found only in God. In these pages, learn what it means to accept and find joy in an alternate way. (152 pages, paperback)

Off Script

Every now and then, God takes our lives off script. He reaches into our circumstances with events we would never choose. These unexpected adventures are often painful, uncomfortable, and scary. This book will help you discover God's heart, God's joy, and God's truth in the fog of an uncertain reality. (240 pages, hardback)

The Burden Bearer

The allegory in these pages will captivate your heart, delight your soul, and profoundly change your life. Follow the main character—Carrier—on his journey with the Burden Bearer, and discover the Christian life and relationship with Jesus that you were meant to enjoy! (184 pages, hardback)

striving together.com

Visit us online

striving together.com

wcbc.edu